WASTE
NOT

'*Waste Not* is a much-needed guidebook for those seeking tangible direction to live a better life. We all know deep down we must change our ways, and fast. Erin shows us how in the most truly responsible way possible – by walking her talk out in front of the movement. I've followed Erin's campaigns and successes for a number of years, and she is a true agent of change.'

SARAH WILSON
New York Times best-selling author
of *I Quit Sugar*

'Erin's blog has been a go-to resource for me ever since I started my own zero waste journey. *Waste Not* combines her wealth of knowledge into an essential, practical guide for anyone looking to reduce their wasteful habits without feeling overwhelmed, offering an alternative to the often "perfect" world of zero waste. Want to break up with single-use plastic? Start with *Waste Not*.'

KATE ARNELL
TV presenter and eco-blogger

'So many people write to me asking how they can go zero waste. It seems people are stuck on where to start. I am so grateful for the existence of *Waste Not* and the foundational work that was laid by Erin to create it. This book contains everything someone would need to start drastically reducing their waste: all the little details that anyone would wonder about, or get stuck on, when it comes to disposing of our wasteful ways and transitioning into a fresh, sustainable and healthy way of being. I give it an A+ – this book really does have it all, including my high recommendation to anyone who's looking to reduce their waste and live a happier and healthier life, whether you've already been on the journey for years, or haven't taken your first step yet.'

ROB GREENFIELD
Environmental activist

ERIN RHOADS

WASTE NOT

MAKE A BIG DIFFERENCE
BY THROWING AWAY LESS

Hardie Grant

BOOKS

INTRODUCTION

'I love being on holiday because you don't have to recycle.'

The year was 2008; I was away on holiday with my extended family, indulging, as always, over Christmas week. I wish I could tell you that directly after making this statement the epiphany arrived that would start me on the journey to writing this book.

Alas readers, it did not. There were many years and many overflowing garbage bins until that particular moment came. Until then, I remained steadfast as an environmentally unfriendly and waste-unaware human being. When my holiday came to a close, my usual lacklustre recycling efforts returned. No-one, not even the person who reminded me of the proclamation I made above, could have predicted I'd go from the poster girl for how to create rubbish to someone who would be asked to talk on the subject of reducing it.

It wasn't a lack of empathy that made me environmentally unconscious. There were other things on my mind; far more important things than what the arrows on the bottom of my plastic containers meant, or knowing where my rubbish went. If all this plastic and overflowing waste were an issue, I thought, surely someone would have fixed it by now? I also believed that if you cared about the environment you had to be a hippie. You couldn't buy heels or like wearing make-up. You wouldn't have a 9-to-5 corporate job and enjoy it. The very idea of watching an eco-documentary bored me. I revelled in the comfortable and convenient life; anything I needed was easy to obtain, wrapped in oodles of packaging that I threw away without a second thought. I was the sort of person who figured that if I tossed something into the recycling bin incorrectly, there was some kind of system in place that would locate the wrong items and remove them. And all the stuff I sent to landfill, well, it would break down eventually.

On reflection, I consider the height of my blindness to be one afternoon when I lived in London. Packing for a festival and in need of a two-person tent, I bought one for £15 from a large retail chain. I didn't think too much about where the tent came from, who had made it or why it was so cheap. All I knew was that it would serve its purpose for the festival and then I'd probably leave it there. Someone would surely collect it and find a use for it, and I could always buy another one for a different festival. And I did, twice!

You might think I'd be cringing at the memory of how wasteful I was, perhaps even chastising myself for my old environmentally unfriendly ways. But I don't really think that's fair. How could I blame someone, even myself, who didn't know better? A lot of us just aren't aware of the issues around growing landfill sites, plastic pollution choking our wildlife or the threat of BPA. If you're not aware of the situation, how can you care enough to make a change?

I mentioned before how boring eco-documentaries are, or, at least, they used to be boring to me. But when my epiphany finally did arrive, it was because of an eco-documentary. It was the middle of June and I was home, sick. I lay in bed, my duvet wrapped around me, sniffling away, dreaming about moving to a small coastal town in North Carolina, when my phone rang. On the other end was my sister checking in to see how I was surviving the worst of head colds. I lamented being stuck inside, the boxes of tissues I was ploughing through, the dismal Melbourne weather and the fact that I had exhausted all my Nicholas Sparks movies. I asked if she had any inspiring movie suggestions; she'd seen a movie called *The Clean Bin Project* and thought I might like it.

After we hung up, I watched the trailer. The premise was a project to not create any rubbish for a year, and part of that was to not buy anything new. I eyed the couple from Canada suspiciously; surely no-one could really avoid creating rubbish? But, with hours to kill until my boyfriend brought me my takeaway dinner, I settled in to watch a fellow redhead named Jen and her partner, Grant, battle it out for who could make the least amount of rubbish.

I never expected this documentary to become a catalyst for change in my life; it was only meant to fill a gap in my afternoon while I convalesced in bed. But my eyes were opened to how much devastation is caused by our throwaway consumer lifestyle. In particular, it was the footage of the Laysan albatross – a bird that I had never so much as even heard of – that left me in tears.

These majestic birds travel to Midway Atoll to become parents on a small stretch of land close to Hawaii. The atoll is not very big, so thousands of birds perch side by side with their young. Sadly, space is the least of their issues; the main threat is plastic. The atoll is in close proximity to the Great Pacific Garbage Patch, where the ocean's currents bring together plastic debris in an area estimated to be about the size of New South Wales – larger than the size of Texas. This is where the adult albatross fish for food for their chicks. Images show the water resembling a thick soup of broken plastic, making it hard for the birds to distinguish between pollution and food.

Adult albatross have no idea they are scooping up manufactured materials that take thousands of years to break down, because, as far as they are concerned, there is no such thing as rubbish. Returning to the atoll, they feed the 'food' to their babies or retain it, stuck in their own stomachs. The babies die from starvation, their little bodies devoid of nutrients but with bellies full of bottle tops, toothbrushes and lighters that they are unable to regurgitate. Thousands of kilograms of plastic are brought back to the atoll by the adult birds every year.

The images of baby albatross stomachs bloated with plastic left me feeling uncomfortable. For days afterwards I couldn't stop thinking about the movie. While I used a lot of plastic, I always put it in a bin; I never purposely polluted or threw things into the ocean. But, for some reason, I now felt this wasn't enough. In a way I was still contributing to the problem by choosing to invest in plastic-packaged everything. My choices were akin to me saying, 'Yes, let's put more plastic into the ocean.' I wanted to do something, but was unsure where to start. So I jumped on the internet, typing in the question 'How can I reduce my plastic use?'

My internet search returned a host of websites, but the one that grabbed my attention was a funny little organisation from Perth, Western Australia, called Plastic Free July. I had heard of Dry July – you know, the month where people give up alcohol while raising money for cancer research – but not a month dedicated to living without single-use plastics. I read the site, learning in more depth some of the facts about plastic and how the choices we make every day can help make to create a more sustainable world.

I signed up, hoping for the best.

For the month of July, I focused on avoiding plastic bags and produce bags, takeaway cups with plastic lids, plastic straws, plastic water bottles, plastic cutlery and plastic takeaway containers. I purchased some reusable shopping bags, asked for my hot chocolate without a lid, practised saying no to straws, chose takeaway food in paper only and that required no plastic cutlery. I set aside a used plastic bag to collect all the plastic I couldn't avoid, otherwise known as my 'dilemma bag'. The dilemma bag helped me identify the offending plastic items that I was having trouble saying no to.

The challenge was harder than I thought. Each day I reminded myself that I was trying to undo twenty-eight years of habits.

At the time, I had a blog to record my travel adventures titled The Rogue Ginger. This space was soon taken over with details about my experiment to live with less plastic. While the challenge was difficult, I was inspired to make changes beyond the everyday plastics. Before I even hit the middle of the month, my plastic-packaged pads and tampons were switched out for reusable cloth pads and a menstrual cup. I still proudly own and use both of these original purchases.

Being aware of my plastic consumption led to a new-found awareness of the benefits of living with less of it. I was eating better, as my shopping trolley mainly consisted of fresh vegetables – the only supermarket aisle where I could find things not wrapped in plastic. I saved time by not having to decipher ingredients on food labels. My 3 pm slump, which had been traditionally alleviated by a processed sweet, was now fixed with fruit. I started saving money as I became more conscious about what, where and who I was opening my wallet for. This also led to a desire to support the local community. I was choosing food and other items grown or made in my own country, not those shipped in by multinational companies more concerned about cheap deals than the conditions under which things were grown or made, let alone the packaging. Life also slowed down as I began to take the time to indulge in moments rather than things. Instead of getting a hot drink to go, I would sit down in the cafe instead, taking ten minutes to enjoy my drink in a ceramic mug. I often thought about all the effort that went into growing our tea and coffee by farmers across the world, handpicking, washing and drying their product, then packaging and sending it across the world to be, more often than not, put into a disposable takeaway cup and drained quickly. Taking time to appreciate it paid respect to the long line of people who made it available to me.

Soon, the last day of July was looming, and while I had not managed to avoid all plastics, I had tried my best. I was happy with my results and the benefits that reducing plastic had brought into my life. I continued to educate myself through documentaries and books while documenting it all on my blog. It was during my search for more information on living with less plastic that I stumbled across Beth Terry, author of the blog My Plastic-Free Life. Like me, Beth had been inspired to change her plastic habits after seeing a photo of a seabird with a belly full of plastic. Her journey – and the fact she still had friends after going plastic-free – inspired me to apply myself to a full-time plastic-free life. I hoped I'd still have friends when I told them.

I soon became a master at explaining to people that I lived a plastic-free life and how this was different from being anti-plastic full stop. I did my best to avoid bringing new plastics into my life but was only anti the misuse and overuse of plastic. I didn't consider plastic used in medicine or for transport a misuse, but a plastic fork or an apple wrapped in plastic? Yes, these were definitely a misuse. I was happy to compromise with some plastic items if I could purchase them second-hand, or if they were an investment for safety or health; for example, I bought a bike with some plastic components. Yep, I bought a bike – so eco! I started composting to avoid plastic bin liners too.

'The Builder', as I creatively nicknamed my boyfriend (who is indeed a builder, and who was later to become my husband), supported my crusade to avoid plastic. Later that year I moved in with him, bringing all my plastic-free swaps with me. We started shopping at bulk stores together, investing in reusable items made of wood, glass or stainless steel, and keeping all old plastic items for other uses. It wasn't always smooth sailing; there were moments of tension and plenty of hiccups. There were times I took the plastic-free lifestyle to the extreme. One fraught day ended in tears when I tried to make worcestershire sauce from scratch. Worcestershire sauce! It was impossible to get from the shops without a plastic lid or the annoying shrink-wrap on the head of the bottle, but it was also – it turns out – pretty impossible to make. I soon had to admit that my obsession with making everything from scratch was not sustainable for my stress levels.

A trip away to Myanmar made me re-evaluate how far I had taken my new lifestyle. On my holiday, I came across individuals and organisations working to reduce plastic in their own way. I realised there that one person's journey is different from another's; it is about doing the best you can, with what you've got, where you are.

I continued doing my best to live plastic-free without burning the house down with my experimental sauce-bottling.

Not long before the end of my first year of living plastic-free, I decided to rewatch *The Clean Bin Project* to reinvigorate and inspire myself. By now, there were some weeks when nothing went into the rubbish bin under our sink. I began looking further into the not just plastic-free but *waste*-free lifestyle, as lived by Jen and Grant. This led me to Anamarie Shreeves, who was living a zero-waste life in Atlanta and blogging about it at Fort Negrita. When I discovered Anamarie, she was measuring the amount of rubbish she was making: in four months, she managed to fit it all inside a small jar. I was blown away! I wondered if I could do the same. I then discovered others like Anamarie, such as Colleen from No Trash Project and Bea Johnson of Zero Waste Home. Bea set up a series of steps known as the five Rs, which can be applied to help reduce how much rubbish individuals send to landfill: *refuse, reduce, reuse, rot* and *recycle*, in that order. I saw many similarities between living plastic-free and zero waste, and I decided to focus not only on my plastic waste but also my landfill contribution. I took the five Rs and adapted them to suit my life, and swapped my bin for an old coffee jar I rescued from my mother-in-law's recycling bin, continuing to write about my efforts to further reduce waste along the way. This was in 2014. Five years on and I am still using the same jar as my rubbish bin without ever having emptied it.

The journey hasn't been easy, but how could it be? I'm trying to live a circular lifestyle in a world that champions throwing things away. A world where companies purposely create items to break down within years so we're forced to buy new ones.

Where things we buy are packaged in plastic because of an assumption about consumer convenience – not actual consumer demand – and because plastic packaging is cheaper for companies to produce and ship. When these items are created or packaged, no-one gives any thought as to where they will end up; money and 'convenience' are more important than the health and welfare of not only the planet, but even the people who make the stuff. Recognising this has lifted much of the guilt I used to feel about waste, because it's not our fault as consumers. But it is something we have the power to change.

Through my pursuit of living plastic-free and with zero waste, I've learned to eat real food, discovered new skills, cut down my exposure to harmful chemicals, found joy in moments instead of things, simplified my life, become more self-sufficient and saved money. I've chosen this lifestyle as it aligns me with intention, kindness and responsibility. And I haven't lost any friends – if anything, it has opened my eyes to a whole new community.

I hope you haven't closed the book after seeing the words 'zero waste'. This book is not just for those who label themselves zero waste; it's for anyone and everyone who'd like to make simple changes where they can to reduce their individual impact and carbon footprint. It doesn't matter whether you are at the beginning of your journey or further along. Zero-waste living is not about fitting waste into a jar; it's about joining a growing group of concerned citizens who want a new system. Our choices can help to shift and mould the world we want for future generations. My intention is not to tell you what to do, but to prove a different way of thinking, interacting and living in this world is possible.

HOW TO USE THIS BOOK

This book is divided into three parts to encourage you to take things slowly. Don't feel you have to make changes immediately and do everything exactly as I have done – remember, this has been a six-year process for me! I encourage you to experiment and explore, adapting what works for your life, not the other way around. It's all about doing the best you can, with what you've got, where you are.

Part One: Tools
This part is all about getting started. The first chapter takes you through why it's so important that we cut down our waste, and breaks down all the lingo around 'zero waste'. Then, in the next chapter, we'll look at the small steps you can take to begin making a difference. This is where I'll introduce you to my *Waste Not* framework and show you how important it is to start with a good mindset, because all the waste in the world is not your fault.

Part Two: Tips
Now it's time to put those tools into action in different areas of your life and home. These chapters are full of hints from my own life, tips from other zero-waste experts, and easy DIYs. At the end of each chapter, you'll find my top tips to take away. Most of these tips aren't radical. Many are similar to what our great-grandparents would've done – it's just a matter of us relearning them.

Part Three: Tricks
This is where we take things to a new level. Zero waste can present some challenges when you're out and about, so we'll look at how you can keep up your new-found habits when you're on holidays, at the park or in the office. Then we'll discuss how you (yes, you) can engage in activism and help spread the *Waste Not* message.

We finish up with my Directory of the products and services that have helped me in transitioning to zero waste, as well as resources that have inspired my journey. I hope they can now help and inspire you!

PART ONE

TOOLS

WHY
WASTE
NOT

In nature there is no such thing as waste.

– David Suzuki

The idea of a system where nothing is wasted is not a new one. From birds, ants, elephants, trees and flowers right down to the microorganisms we can't see, there is no waste. Every action by these plants and creatures is utilised somehow in a circular system. A branch falls from a tree; over time the branch is broken down by microorganisms and fungi, feeding nutrients into the soil that aid the growth of new plants; these plants are food for animals and become their shelters and birthplaces until a time when the plant will come to the end of its life and the cycle will start again.

> **Fact**
>
> Australia is the second-largest producer of waste per capita in the world, behind the US.

Not too long ago, humans also lived within a circular system but, following the Industrial Revolution, the paradigm began to shift as we discovered how to make goods on a larger scale. The speed of developing technologies erupted, hurtling us from the circular system and dropping us onto the linear conveyor belt we are stuck on today. We use powerful machines running on fossil fuels to extract resources from the ground and ship them across the world where we mould and shape them into products in large factories on mass scales. These products are then sent to stores where we buy them; we then send the product to landfill – and repeat.

Every action has a reaction. The choices we make have a ripple effect, upstream and downstream. In fact, I'm yet to find any threat facing our environment and animals that is not a direct result of our misguided use of natural resources. A majority of the waste created is classed as industrial, meaning it is waste left over from the mining and processing of resources into the stuff we buy. Fuel, whether it is oil, gas or coal, is required for all activities. The solar panels that are supposed to save us still require finite resources. I read over and over about the desperate need to swap from coal to solar as a way of dealing with the issues of climate change. But reducing our consumption levels is just as important.

To put it simply, the more stuff we buy and the more new items we bring into our homes, the more energy is needed to keep the machines running, factory lights on, trucks rolling, trains running and ships sailing. The less stuff we need to make, the less strain we'll be putting on the planet.

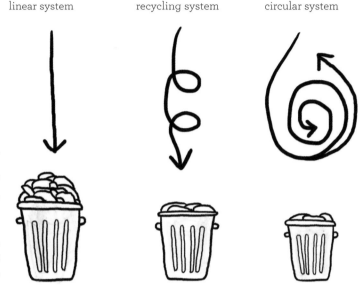

linear system   recycling system   circular system

The waste we create is largely planned at the start of a product cycle, in the design process. Sadly, waste is almost purposely created to encourage us to buy over and over and over again; the idea even has a name: planned obsolescence. A product is designed to fail without a thought as to where it will end up; the purpose is to keep people returning to the store to buy a new one. The low prices trick us into replacing a product rather than repairing it. The more affordable a product, the greater the chance it was made with poor materials and in dire conditions by people paid a small wage.

The mentality of easy replacement has seeped further afield, where we replace something even before it is broken, driven by a need to keep up with the Joneses or from fear of missing out. And the recycling system has become a bandaid solution that doesn't do anything to curb our consumption.

Our passivity in the face of the making-and-throwing-away cycle has become deeply ingrained. It makes me wonder if we are ready to face the fact that consumption is the root cause of so many problems. But we need to realise this, in order to see that we have the potential to make change.

THE IMPACT OF WASTE

When I share the reasons why I am passionate about reducing waste, I usually talk about three things:

☐ the damage from plastic

☐ ocean pollution

☐ our toxic landfill sites

I mention the impact that these have on our environment and our health. But then there is also the impact on people – communities I've never ventured to; women, men and children I'll never meet. My role as a mindless consumer encouraged corporations to continue taking advantage of communities who have been forced to move from their lands or work in factories. My purchases were part of a supply chain that endangered people's health in unfair working environments, and the health of people living beside these factories, where the cheapest housing can often be found. It has a flow-on effect to parts of the world where people are forced to live in or around garbage sites, or to make a living from scavenging through broken glass and rotting food in landfills to find something worth selling. The irony is that many of the people in these situations are living some of the zero-waste practices mentioned throughout this book, but out of necessity.

> **Fact**
> The pollution from fossil fuels is estimated to contribute to 19,000 deaths every day.

PLASTIC

Plastic takes an incredibly long time to break down, with estimates from 500 to thousands of years. What we do know is that every single bit of plastic made in the last century still exists somewhere today. While most plastics are considered recyclable, it hasn't stopped plastic from getting into the environment. Unlike less manufactured materials, nothing plastic is returned to the soil for nourishment, food or life. It will sit around clogging up landfills or end up in our rivers, oceans, forests and deserts. Scientists are now finding plastic particles in the air we breathe and the water we drink, even in beer, honey and table salt.

The manufacturing of plastic has a heavy impact on the environment, polluting air, soil and ground water. Not only are plastics made from oil, but they require the use of fossil fuels, which are non-renewable resources, to power their manufacture. Then there are the resources and waste associated with shipping plastics such as nurdles (plastic pellets before they become, for example, a single-use plastic spoon) around the world.

I'm not anti-plastic, simply anti its misuse. The use of plastic in medicine has allowed for greater accessibility, inventions and progress to help alleviate symptoms and cure diseases. Plastic-packaged mustard, on the other hand, doesn't do any of those things.

Not all plastics are the same. If you know your plastics, you can probably put your hand up and tell me there are seven different categories of plastics that we use every day, all of which have been linked to damaging environmental and health outcomes.

1: Polyethylene terephthalate (PETE or PET) features in plastic drink bottles, cosmetic packaging, polyester clothing and homewares like carpet and furniture. PET is the most commonly recycled plastic and considered one of the safest. However, the US Food and Drug Administration (FDA) have determined that all plastics leach no matter what. For instance, PETE or PET has been shown to break down into the contents of bottles that have been reused.

2: High-density polyethylene (HDPE) is used to make other types of plastic bottles, as well as milk jugs, toys and water pipes. HDPE is usually firmer than other plastics and, like PETE or PET, is one of the 'safer' plastics. But it's still made from a non-renewable resource and pollutes the environment.

3: Vinyl or polyvinyl chloride (V or PVC) is up there with polystyrene as the most toxic and hazardous of all the plastics. It is made up of dioxins, vinyl chloride and phthalates. Dioxins are known carcinogens, also causing development problems and reproductive issues. Vinyl chloride is linked to ground and water pollution, cancer and liver, lung and kidney damage. Phthalates are endocrine disruptors, linked to abnormal foetal development and breast and testicular cancer; some studies are looking at a link to autism too. You'll find PVC in children's toys, plastic wrap, rain jackets and shower curtains. Of all the plastics,

PVC lets off the most toxic chemicals into the air, particularly as items get older.

4: Low-density polyethylene (LDPE) is used to make plastic bags, milk cartons, the lining in cardboard food packaging, food storage containers and a covering for electrical wires. Its flexibility makes it the most popular plastic used. Like HDPE, it also poses a lower health threat but this does not mean it is completely safe. Especially when used at high temperatures, it will release chemicals that may affect our hormones. LDPE can be collected for recycling but is often only recycled once before it can no longer be recycled again (otherwise known as *down-cycling*).

5: Polypropylene (PP) is found in disposable nappies, menstrual pads, single-use food containers and household items like cups and plates. Originally it was considered a 'safe' plastic but has since been found to leach substances known to disrupt our brain receptors.

6: Polystyrene (PS) can be either expanded (like Styrofoam) or rigid, and is used for foam cups and food packaging, toys and disposable cutlery. It is made using styrene, which is considered toxic to the nervous system and carcinogenic. When expanded into foam, the material breaks up readily, allowing it to move about more easily in the environment and, therefore, cause more destruction.

7: Other: this category includes plastics made of polycarbonate (PC), which can contain bisphenol A (BPA). PC is often used in babies' bottles, DVDs and CDs, mobile phone cases and food packaging, including to line food tins to stop the metal from leaching into the food – but instead, the plastic can leach into the food. BPA and its substitutes (bisphenol S or F) have been found to affect the immune system, impair neurological function and increase the risk of diabetes as well as breast, prostate and testicular cancer. BPA has been banned for use in some children's toys and food containers, but can still be found on our receipts, in dental fillings and in paint. In fact, BPA global production is more than four million tones per year, making it one of the highest-volume chemicals manufactured. The more often PC items are used, whether hot or cold, old or new, BPA will leach out.

OCEAN POLLUTION

Like many, learning of the Laysan albatross and the Great Pacific Garbage Patch was what put me on the road to looking at my own life and how I could help. But they're far from the only ocean wildlife impacted by waste. Sea turtles have been found with forks and straws stuck in their noses, their bellies full of plastic bags that they mistook for jellyfish. Much of the plastic entering our oceans doesn't even make it to the Great Pacific Garbage Patch; instead, it's slowly covering the ocean floor. There is no place on this planet untouched by plastic; it's been washing up on the most remote beaches in the world and sinking to the deepest sea trenches.

While plastic can take a long time to break down, it doesn't take as long to break up. Sunlight, water and wind weaken plastic to the point where it will break into smaller pieces or 'microplastics': fragments of plastic measuring less than 5 mm (0.2 in). Microplastics are the kind of plastics that are brought together into large concentrations like the Great Pacific Garbage Patch by ocean currents around the world. Another plastic culprit is the microbead: little plastic balls found in face scrubs and toothpaste. Created to act as exfoliators, they are washed down the sink when used and are so tiny that they can't be filtered by the water treatment facilities. Another sneaky plastic making its way into the ocean is microfibre. Synthetic clothes, like polyester, release synthetic fibres when we wash and wear them, and these tiny fibres eventually get into waterways leading to the ocean.

Unsurprisingly, all of these tiny pieces of plastic are now being found in the seafood we eat. In 2016, some scientists found that Europeans could consume more that 11,000 pieces of microplastic per year through seafood. Plastic acts as a magnet, attracting persistent organic pollutants (POPs), dioxins, industrial fallouts, oil and heavy metals. Some of these substances come from waste created upstream during production or are simply in our cleaning and beauty products. This means that when we are inadvertently consuming plastic, it's not only plastic but other hazardous chemicals – even DDT, which was banned decades ago but still lingers in our oceans. If we don't curb our consumption, an ocean with more plastic than fish will be a reality by 2050.

LANDFILL SITES

Landfill is a business. Money is made from the collection and burying of our stuff. Rubbish that is put out on the street moves away from our lives but does not go away, because there is no *away*. It is merely transported to the outskirts of our cities to sit around for eons, taking up land and never truly breaking down. Landfills can leach dangerous chemicals and create harmful gas – and that's not mentioning the smell (though in my opinion, landfills don't smell as bad as recycling facilities, but that could be due to the weird sprays used to help hide the stench).

Our landfills create a toxic sludgy run-off called *leachate*. When it rains, water works its way through the layers of our rubbish, collecting all the hazardous chemicals from our cleaning products, discarded batteries, paints, pesticides, rotted food waste and electronics, and carries everything down into the soil surrounding the landfill before making its way into groundwater. Newer landfill sites are engineered to collect and remove the leachate but, unfortunately, the system is not perfect and old landfill sites are harder to manage. Once the leachate enters our groundwater, there is no way of removing it.

Chemicals don't only make their way out of landfills via water; they also escape through the air. A lot of the rubbish in our landfills has the potential to emit harmful volatile organic compounds (VOCs). In our homes, we are exposed to VOCs from the paint on our walls and the cleaners and protectors sprayed on our furniture and clothing. Over time, the VOCs coming from our possessions reduce, but with the continual growth of landfills, more and more VOCs offgas in the air.

One particular VOC is methane gas, one of the major greenhouse gases. This is a by-product of all the organics (food scraps, paper, cardboard, garden trimmings) we waste in landfill. When our plastic bags of rubbish are thrown into landfill, bags are layered upon each other, then covered with dirt. The process is repeated over and over each week. The resulting density creates an imbalance; the food rots slowly into a liquid rather than breaking down, creating methane in the process. Some landfill sites capture methane and burn it as fuel (methane is the main component in natural gas). Burning our waste to create energy is a disputed topic; more and more people are concerned that it is a toxic air-polluting bandaid to a bigger problem, and that problem is waste.

> **Fact**
> Each year more than 500,000 tonnes of textiles end up in Australian landfill sites.

THE POTENTIAL FOR CHANGE

You might think that this sounds all doom and gloom, and you're right: some of this information is depressing. But that's not to say there isn't change happening. You've picked up this book; perhaps you are making changes already. I can honestly say you are not alone – *we* are not alone. There is a growing swell of individuals coming together to say that our earth's resources are too precious to be used to make a disposable plastic fork.

Down the road from me there is a group of neighbours who meet up to sew shopping bags from salvaged cloth to give away in local shops. Children as young as ten are starting clean-up groups in their parks, petitioning local governments to stop the free handout of plastic straws and even asking their school canteens to do away with plastic cutlery. Choices like these, made with kindness and compassion, are felt for generations beyond our own.

Even big businesses are making changes. Sierra Nevada Brewing Co. in California actively creates a circular system in their product processes, diverting 99.8 per cent of total solid waste from landfill. BMW has worked at reducing the variety of plastics in its cars to make them easier to recycle into new car parts. The Cradle to Cradle Products Innovation Institute has been set up to change the way designers and manufacturers make products. The staff at the institute work closely with companies to ensure they meet their strict product standards. There are many more stories of businesses trying to undo the mess we are in.

As individuals, we have direct control over our choices. Participating in a zero-waste lifestyle sends messages in every direction, putting pressure on the companies upstream to do better, to rethink the system and to continue looking forwards.

ZERO WASTE?

There is a multitude of terms used to describe those who have resolved to cut back on the materials they cram into their bins each week. The terms may be different but at the heart of each is the collective desire to live in a world where no resource is wasted.

By definition, 'zero waste' is about imitating the natural world, where there is no such thing as a waste of resources. In a zero-waste world, everything we create would have a continual use and there would be no need for landfills or incinerators filled with toxic waste.

Zero waste was originally an industrial term, used to describe a system that creates little to no rubbish during product design. The term was invented by a California-based chemist, Dr Paul Palmer, in the mid-1970s. His company, Zero Waste Systems Inc. (ZWS), was set up after he discovered many of the new electronic businesses in Silicon Valley were sending industrial chemicals that still had a use to landfill. His company was the first of its kind to identify ways of diverting chemical waste from landfill and begin saving it and selling it on to other companies. Soon enough, Palmer and ZWS gained global attention. Palmer began looking at systems outside chemicals, applying what he had learned on ways to reduce waste in other areas. This led to the founding of the Zero Waste Institute, based on his belief that there should be a use for every by-product before production even begins. Palmer identified waste as a design flaw and saw recycling as a short-term solution for items that still inevitably ended up in landfill. *Planning* for zero waste was the ideal approach to creating a new system.

Decades after Palmer coined the term 'zero waste' came another Californian resident, Bea Johnson, who would also gain global attention for waste-reduction practices. Where Palmer focused on redesigning products at the start of their life to enable zero waste, Bea Johnson showed on her blog and later book, *Zero Waste Home*, how everyday people could rebel against waste by looking at the rubbish they produced in their own homes. She was the first to set up a framework – the five Rs – that people like you and me could apply to our lifestyles as a way to enable waste minimisation in the home. Like Palmer, Johnson also came to realise recycling was simply a way to delay what would end up in landfill.

Fact

My journey to zero-waste living started with 'plastic-free' living. Within the realms of modern society, plastic-free living is more about reducing reliance on the material and trying to not bring virgin (new) plastic into our lives. The emphasis is on *try*.

'Circular living' and 'pre-cycling' are like Palmer's definition of zero waste, with a focus on preventing the creation of waste during the design of the product. 'Low waste' and 'minimal waste' are the same as Johnson's idea of zero waste: using the five Rs philosophy to reduce waste going to landfill.

I adopted the label 'zero waste' simply because I had not yet heard of any other lifestyle labels for a set of values based on creating less waste. Some people find the word 'zero' – or even 'circular' – polarising, and others find it misleading. In our present system, waste is created when a product we use is made. Whether it's during the extraction of resources from the ground, the growing of ingredients, the production process, transporting the product, even the design of the machines that put these products together – every step creates waste.

I interpret someone living a zero-waste, circular, pre-cycling, low-waste or minimal-waste lifestyle as one trying their best to reduce, as much as possible, the amount of rubbish they send to landfill by following a set of principles. I'll never be completely zero waste; there is no way for this to happen until the system changes from a linear to a circular one. But I can participate in a zero-waste lifestyle and divert as much rubbish from landfill as I thoughtfully can.

Many of the steps in this book are not new or revolutionary. There are cultures and people who have practiced these methods of managing resources as a way of life, and many still do. But for most of the western industrialised world these practices have been forgotten. To participate in the zero-waste lifestyle as I do is not only a response to mounting landfill sites and the litter choking our environment and animals, but also to protect people who are directly impacted by our overconsumption.

Being able to redesign the system at the top, as envisioned by Dr Paul Palmer, is the holy grail of zero waste. Many of us don't have the ability or time to address every company on ways to redesign its products. But, like Bea Johnson, we do have the power to engage in change by choosing where and how we buy things. If companies see more and more people demanding a different system through their purchases, then Palmer's vision of zero waste could still become a reality.

WHAT ABOUT RECYCLING?

Recycling is a labour-intensive process requiring energy and fuel, and most of it is not done in our country. Until recently, China was the world's largest importer of recyclable materials. In 2013, a campaign was set up called Green Fence, focused on returning recycling to countries that don't properly clean and sort their materials; China had been sending this contaminated recycling – which often hid highly toxic materials – to landfill. In 2017, China made the decision to halt the import of recycling material entirely in order to focus on improving its own environmental practices rather than become a dumping ground for the rest of the world. The move sent a shock wave through the recycling industry, which relied on China to deal with what local markets could not.

You might be surprised to know most of the recycling you diligently placed in your bins was, for a long time, sent to China; I know I was. The thing is that recycling, like landfill, is a business – a complex enterprise driven by market values and the demand for material. When the price is low, or the market is overwhelmed by a material, the stock can sit for months until the price is high enough for the recycling company to gain a profit. Yes, that's right: our recycling makes money.

There is also the misconception that what we put into our recycling bins will be recycled indefinitely or even recycled at all, an issue caused by lack of information and the varying symbols on products. You might think that the chasing arrows symbol means that the material will be recycled over and over, but this is not the case. The symbol simply means that the material *can* be recycled or that it has recycled content in it. Many plastics, for example, are often down-cycled, meaning they will become just one more object before that material reaches the end of its life. For many of the items we send off for recycling, they are merely one product away from landfill.

Let's step back and look at the process of kerbside recycling. Metal, paper, certain glass and some plastics are collected regularly. The trucks remove the contents to a materials recovery facility where everything is sorted by material and baled up. From here, it's sent to another facility to either be broken down into a new material that can be recycled, or it's sent further afield to complete this process – it all depends on the material.

> **Fact**
> China once took in over 85 per cent of the world's recycling, including from Australia, the USA and some European countries.

☐ Metal (think a tin can) has a higher value and is rarely left sitting around. The cost and energy needed to recycle metal are lower than in making virgin metal. Metal also has the added bonus of being able to be recycled continually if the material is not contaminated.

☐ Paper also has a high value, but this can fluctuate. Unlike metal, paper and cardboard can only be recycled up to ten times before the fibres become too weak for reuse.

☐ Since the demand for recycled glass is low and requires diligent sorting by colour – which many facilities don't do due to cost – glass is currently more likely to be recycled into sand for construction projects.

☐ Due to the continued rise in plastic packaging around the world, there is a bottomless pit of plastic waiting to be recycled.

I'd like to make it clear I'm not advocating against recycling; the process is an important part of our present waste-management system, diverting precious resources from landfill. My goal is to simply point out how flawed the recycling business is, to show you we can't get to zero waste by recycling. For the system to change, the people who make our goods need to make things that can be recycled easily and continually (a jar is turned back into a jar) and to also choose recycled materials for use. Think about a commercial perfume bottle. The product is made of a complex mix of materials – glass, plastic and metal – which would all need to be separated in order to be recycled. It is up to the companies who design these bottles to make a product that can be recycled.

Being the pragmatic optimist that I am, I hope China's decision to reduce the amount of recycling it imports will be a wake-up call to develop new systems. It should encourage us to put more thought into the development of products, to consider their reuse, and to take responsibility for the recycling and other waste we produce locally. I could fill this book on why recycling is not the answer; instead I have listed some of my favourite books on the topic in the Directory (page 262).

THE WASTE NOT FRAMEWORK

For my first year of living zero waste, I had stuck on my fridge my own framework modelled on Bea Johnson's five Rs; being a visual person, seeing the framework every day in a prominent spot acted as a handy reminder. Since no two lives are the same and we all live in different locations in varying circumstances, make your own framework to suit your life. Of course, there is no need for a set of rules or a framework at all – find what works for you.

REDESIGN. With 80 per cent of a product's impact determined at the concept phase, I don't hold back on sending things back to a company with suggestions on how to create a smarter product or more sustainable packaging. Don't be afraid to speak up if something you've owned or seen is wasteful.

RETHINK what you buy and what you throw away.

REFUSE the unnecessary stuff and poorly designed systems. Just because something is free doesn't mean we can't say no. After all, saying no is also free.

REUSE, and choose items that can be reused, over and over again. Before recycling anything or sending it to landfill, ask yourself: what could the life of this product be? It could be as simple as reusing a glass bottle for food storage or reimagining it as something else: a vase, a candle holder or even a light fitting.

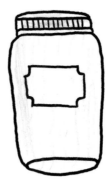

REDUCE meaningless waste by removing items from your life that no longer serve you but could be useful to someone else. Question if the stuff you want to bring into your life makes things easier or if it is just cumbersome.

SHARE resources, food, talent and possessions with your communities. Sharing what we already own and borrowing what we don't changes the story on what we see as waste.

REPAIR the goods you own, whether by learning the skills to mend them or by supporting individuals and organisations who can. Companies should see the need to make items that are repairable.

COMPOST by choosing materials as close to nature as possible and setting up practices where these natural goods can be disposed of properly.

RECYCLE when the previous steps are unavoidable – but make sure to do it correctly, and if in doubt, leave it out.

CHOOSE KINDNESS. Being mindful and conscious with the stuff we buy, how we buy it and how we treat it has a knock-on effect.

BE THE CHANGE and be proud of your efforts, big and small. They all add weight to worldwide change.

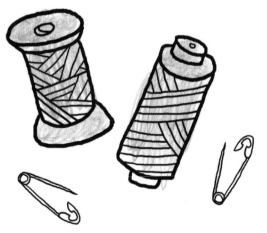

DON'T
FORGET
THE
REUSABLE
BAGS

WHERE TO START

The purpose of this book is to share ways to reduce our personal waste – after all, this is the area where we have the most control. But making personal changes can still be hard. It wouldn't be fair or honest if I said adopting a low-waste lifestyle was easy and will happen within thirty days. I'm also not saying it's *too* hard, but there will be some emotional speed humps you'll encounter when, for example, you are trying to cut down on single-use plastics but no-one else around you is. The low-waste lifestyle is a circular lifestyle, but society is currently built on a linear system. I liken it to the round-peg-square-hole metaphor, except instead of putting the round peg into a square hole, it's thrown into the square bin. Before launching into where to start, I think getting into the right mindset is very important.

DON'T SUCCUMB TO ENVIRONMENTAL GUILT

When I began to make changes to create less waste, I'd have days where I'd forget to say no to a plastic straw or I couldn't find a low-waste option for a food item I was trying to replace. Every time something like this happened, I felt like a failure. It's so easy to become fixated on where we make mistakes, when we should be celebrating our wins. Refusing something like a plastic bag three times in a row and then forgetting on the fourth attempt does not mean your efforts are doomed and you should give up because that one forgetful moment will lead to the destruction of humankind.

This, my friend, is environmental guilt or eco-guilt. It's when you feel the need to be the perfect eco-warrior, changing everything in your life immediately, donating money to this and that cause, and it all becomes too much, yet you feel like you're still not doing enough . . . Remember, you are not solely to blame for climate change, the plastic in the oceans and growing landfill sites. When you are overwhelmed like this, it just creates anger and frustration, leading you to throwing in the (reusable) towel.

DON'T BE TOO HARD ON YOURSELF

I can assure you the more you delve into a low-waste life, the more you will become inundated with information, and with that information, a set of standards too. There are books, blogs, websites, forums, Facebook pages, Instagram feeds – all with their own way of being plastic-free or zero waste or both. Seek them out, learn from them, ask questions, but none of these sources of information should be seen as measuring sticks. The trick here is to set your own standards. Let's remember: it's about doing the best you can, with what you've got, where you are.

My number-one piece of advice to anyone starting this journey is to never compare yourself to someone else. We are all unique individuals on different paths, living different lives. Location, time, money, accessibility: all play a part in the decisions we make.

Allow for time. Weeks. Months. Years. Go at your own pace and figure out what works for you; it's not a race. Not everyone's rubbish has to fit into a box or a jar. If you can't get ingredients in bulk to make your own deodorant, don't fret. Explore your options and find your own solution. Comparing yourself to others will only hold you back and stop you from seeing what you can achieve.

DON'T FORCE YOUR STANDARDS ON OTHERS

I used to get angry when I saw people walking out of supermarkets with their double-bagged plastic bags full of plastic-packaged food, or get upset if friends around me were using plastic or not caring about the waste they were creating. Fortunately, I was quick to realise that holding onto this anger was useless; it was a waste of my energy. It wasn't fair to chastise people who might not know better. Instead, I redirected my energy towards myself and my own behaviour, choosing to lead by example.

But it can also be isolating to pursue a zero-waste lifestyle alone. I began surrounding myself, offline and online, with like-minded people who became my allies. It was in these groups that I learned to channel the frustration I used to feel into meaningful contributions through community action. Knowing there were other people out there with the same passion gave me the confidence to engage in my own form of activism, which didn't include chaining myself to a building or storming a local meeting. Activism is a wonderful expression of resistance and rebellion. As we'll explore in Part Three, there are many ways to – as I like to say – 'act your vision': to create wider change beyond the personal without forcing your standards on others.

DON'T FORGET TO MAKE IT FUN

While choosing to create less rubbish and saying no to unnecessary plastic is serious, I do implore you to try to make the process fun. As I said before, change can be difficult, but finding joy and keeping it fun will make the transition easier. I found a lot of the challenges I faced in reducing waste were easier to deal with when met with playfulness, as it provided more creative solutions. I hope that through this book you'll come across many ways to examine, explore and experiment while keeping it fun.

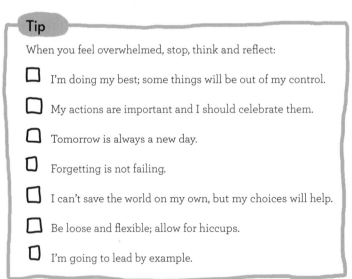

Tip

When you feel overwhelmed, stop, think and reflect:

☐ I'm doing my best; some things will be out of my control.

☐ My actions are important and I should celebrate them.

☐ Tomorrow is always a new day.

☐ Forgetting is not failing.

☐ I can't save the world on my own, but my choices will help.

☐ Be loose and flexible; allow for hiccups.

☐ I'm going to lead by example.

THE SINGLE-USE PLASTIC CHALLENGE

The best way to kick off a journey to reducing waste is by starting with your single-use plastic footprint. Plastic is one of the worst types of waste; if all you do is reduce your plastic waste, you are still making a significant change. The oceans and their creatures, our land environment and future generations will all be better off for it. A plastic-free challenge also eases you into making changes slowly without becoming too overwhelmed, and helps you find a groove for getting into the habit of refusing and reusing.

Amazingly, the single-use plastic challenge mainly consists of switching out just seven frequently used items (or six categories, if you're being technical). Each of these has been designed for just one use, but they all have a simple swap.

☐ plastic shopping bags and produce bags

☐ plastic water bottles   ☐ plastic coffee cups

☐ plastic straws   ☐ plastic cutlery

☐ plastic takeaway containers

For two weeks (or longer), just pretend these items don't exist. I suggest keeping a box or old plastic bag to collect any cups or bottles or bags that slip through. This helps you identify what single-use plastics you still use and how to reduce them. Once you have a bit more confidence, it will be easier to hand stuff back, like straws and cutlery. These will probably still be thrown away but at least you are sending a message that single-use plastics are not needed. Another method is to build up slowly: for example, say no to plastic bags for two weeks, then move on to water bottles, working your way down the list. If two weeks seems too short, stretch it out to a month or three! You get to make the rules.

SHOPPING BAGS
+ PRODUCE BAGS

Human beings have shopped for thousands of years without plastic
shopping bags; in fact, they have only been in existence since the
1960s. Before the flimsy bags came into our lives, cloth bags, woven
jute bags, baskets, boxes and paper bags were all common choices.
Most of us have some form of reusable bag stuffed away in cupboards.
I use a range of bags that I've collected over the years, from ones that
roll up to fit in my handbag or The Builder's pocket, to baskets gifted
by friends and even the reusable bags from supermarkets. If we are
ever without our shopping bags, we will ask for a box or paper bag
(sometimes those mushroom bags work perfectly), or use our hands.
Friends of mine use shopping trolleys or backpacks too.

   Plastic produce bags are not needed either; reusable bags are
again a simple alternative. We use drawstring cloth bags up-cycled
from leftover material. I've also seen people make produce bags
from old curtain netting. Otherwise there are many brands selling
lightweight produce bags – check online or at your local bulk store.
Most of our fruit and vegetables do not require bagging; bananas,
avocados, pumpkins and oranges, for example, all come with their
own natural packaging. Most of us wash our fruit and vegetables
when we take them home anyway.

WATER BOTTLES

There are many different types of reusable bottles available; again, these could already be hiding in your cupboards. I prefer using stainless steel as it is least likely to have a lining of plastic in it the way an aluminum bottle will. If you would prefer not to purchase a new water bottle, try second-hand stores or reuse a glass juice bottle. Some bottles will have built-in filtration, if this is something you'd like. When you're out, fill up at drinking fountains or visit a cafe or restaurant – I have had no trouble asking for my bottle to be filled up for free when I need it. With a bottle tucked away in your bag, you will realise how silly paying for bottled water is.

COFFEE CUPS

Full disclosure: I don't drink coffee. The smell is amazing but one sip and I'd be out with a migraine. So while my morning does not begin with a coffee, many others' mornings do, like The Builder's (he loves a long black). A simple swap is to take ten minutes and sit in to have your coffee in a mug. You are so worth that ten minutes! The Builder swears coffee tastes better in a ceramic mug anyway.

If you are wanting to get your coffee to go and think saying no to the plastic lid is enough, just remember that the lining of paper cups is also made of plastic – a thin film of the same plastic used to make plastic bags. The Builder has a reusable coffee cup in his car and also keeps a regular mug from home on his worksite, plus others for any tradespeople working on the day (I did wonder where all our mugs went to). He has tried steel, glass and silicone reusable coffee cups and thinks all three are better than the single-use coffee cups available. They all come with lids, so there is no risk of any leftover coffee getting into your bag. When taking your own reusable cup, ask to see if the coffee store will give you a discount.

Tip

The WeTap app tells you where to find public drinking fountains all over the world. Paris now even has sparkling water fountains!

Fact

Australians use one billion disposable coffee cups each year.

STRAWS

Plastic straws are one of the top ten items found during coastal clean-ups. Saying no to plastic straws takes practice. Here is a handy tip: when the waiter takes your order, ask them to write down your request for no straw, just like if you were asking for no ice. Some drinks call for straws, so why not invest in a reusable straw made of stainless steel, bamboo, silicone or glass? I carry one around with me (along with a wooden spoon, fork and knife), but if I am without it, I simply ask for a spoon to help me with thicker drinks like smoothies or milkshakes.

CUTLERY

I mentioned above that I carry around a wooden spoon, fork and knife, but this is not the only way to avoid plastic cutlery. Choose an eatery with regular metal cutlery or, if you are getting takeaway at work, grab utensils from the work kitchen and wrap them in a tea towel (dish towel) for use outside the office. You could even carry cutlery from home the same way. I prefer wooden cutlery as it is lighter and can be used on airlines.

TAKEAWAY CONTAINERS

I kept a reusable container in my desk drawer at work for three years, using it to collect my lunch on Fridays (my treat day). I asked local eateries to place sushi, dumplings, nachos, sandwiches, rice paper rolls, whatever I felt like, in it. I never had an issue; usually the people behind the counter would say it was a good idea, commenting on how if everyone did it the business would save a lot of containers (and money). Most days I made my own lunch and took it into work in a reusable container, glass jar or beeswax wrap. If I ever forgot my container, I'd ask the eatery if they had a plate or bowl, claiming I had a 'sensitivity' to takeaway plastic containers. It always worked!

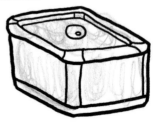

TIPS TO REMEMBER YOUR REUSABLES

As you can see, there are plenty of replacements for all these plastic items, many of which existed well before plastic came along – hundreds of years before! What I needed was a way to remember them. According to James Clear, writer on behavioural psychology and habit formation, every habit we have follows a pattern known as the three Rs of habit change: *reminder*, *routine* and *reward*. The reward for me was using less plastic. The tools to start the routine were readily available. It was the reminder, the first step in the pattern, that needed the most work.

Electronic reminders

Most people these days have smartphones or some kind of device that will send electronic reminders. During my first plastic-free challenge, I spent an hour putting reminders into my phone and email calendars, setting up events with phrases such as 'don't forget your water bottle', 'put your reusable bags in your handbag', 'say no to plastic bags', 'don't get a straw in your drink at the pub tonight', and 'sit in and enjoy your tea'. My phone would beep throughout the day. After a month, the constant repetition of reminders had become so ingrained that I began consciously asking myself if I had my water bottle or cloth bag before I left the house.

Visual reminders

I would usually hang my cloth bag on the front door so I would see it before I left the house. Did I forget from time to time? I wouldn't be human if I didn't. But by getting into the routine of rehanging the bag each time, it became something I just expected to see. I also stuck notes on my handbag, the fridge and anywhere that I passed by during the week. I even had one in my wallet. It might be daggy or cumbersome to put notes about the house or into your phone. But it's not forever. As each day moved along, the reminders helped me to action new habits that did eventually become my new normal.

Tip

Make a hanger for your front door or rear-view mirror to remind yourself as you're leaving the house – there's one to print out on my website.

NEWSPAPER BIN LINER

I hear so often how people use the plastic bags from the shops as bin liners. The thing is, the average household uses 440 plastic bags per year. If our bins are emptied each week, then we only need 52 bags for our bins per year, meaning you'd still be left with 388 plastic bags. By switching to newspaper, there is less chance of polluting the environment and the wildlife that call it home. If you read your news on-screen, ask local cafes or even your local newsagency for newspapers they no longer use.

Lay four sheets of newspaper out and trim to form a square.

Fold down the top left corner to the opposite corner, forming a triangle.

Fold corner 1 over, reaching between corners 2 and 3.

Fold corner 3 over.

Gather two of the flaps on corner 2, folding down the front.

Repeat with the other two, folding down the reverse side.

Congratulations, you made a plastic-free bin liner! Open up the pouch and place it in your bin.

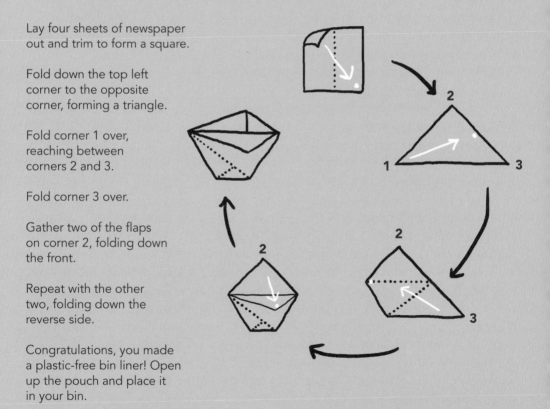

WHAT AM I THROWING AWAY?

As you gain confidence in refusing single-use plastics, and the habits of reusing become easier, you might be feeling ready to expand the challenge. I know taking smaller steps works well for me and others I've worked with over the years. The next step I encourage people to take before reducing waste in other areas of their lives is to conduct a bin audit.

Reading those words naturally conjures up images of sorting through your bin but, I assure you, it's not as messy as that. A bin audit allows you to understand what is being thrown away and what area of your life produces the most waste.

Take a piece of recycled paper or open an on-screen document and divide it into four sections. Label the squares with these headings:

edible food and scraps	plastic (plastic food packaging, bottles, toiletries, etc.)
other packaging (cardboard, tin, etc.)	other

Before throwing anything into your bin, write the offending item on the piece of paper. For example, a limp carrot or leftovers go in the edible food and scraps square, the plastic packaging of frozen vegetables or biscuits would go in the plastic square, and so on.

When you are living a zero-waste life, recycling is also considered waste and many people like to reduce the amount of material they put out for recyling too, so if you would also like to tackle this area, then you can do a recycling bin audit as well: use another piece of recycled paper or a document and divide it into four sections, labelling each 'plastic', 'glass', 'paper' and 'metal'. If that seems too much (I know it would have for me at the beginning), come back and conduct a recycling bin audit later.

At the end of two weeks, you should see a pattern of where the most amount of waste is being created: usually this is edible food and scraps (unless you compost already) and plastic from food packaging. I hope your plastics will already be down from the single-use plastic challenge, but it might have made you notice how much plastic is everywhere!

Looking at the waste created, you might feel overwhelmed as to where to start cutting down. One idea is to choose a square to focus on and work your way around to the others eventually. Since our bins are mostly filled up with food scraps, I advise starting there by looking into composting and learning tricks to become more savvy with food waste from the Kitchen + Food chapter of this book.

Now you have a list of what you're putting into your bin, it's also a good idea to double-check that you are putting everything into the *right* bins. There might be some plastics in your garbage bin that could go into your recycling bin, or you might be able to put food scraps into your green waste bin. Councils offer robust and detailed information about waste through different programs (workshops, tours of recycling and waste facilities and other events) and websites – or you can email or call to arrange for the correct information to be sent out to you. Each council handles waste and recycling differently, so if you are in doubt about an item, ask them first.

Fact

Cardboard food packaging used for milk, juice, ice cream or cream usually contains an invisible layer of plastic either on the inside of the container or compressed between two pieces of cardboard. This plastic is discarded to landfill when the packaging is recycled.

PLASTIC AUDIT

Now, let's put it all together! You can use a plastic audit to keep track of what plastic or plastic-packaged items you are still throwing away and could replace with alternatives. Take another piece of recycled paper (or a document) and divide it into two columns. In column A write down the disposable plastic you have in your house. Use column B to list alternatives with little to no plastic. It's also a good idea to add where they can be purchased for future reference and how to dispose of them without going to landfill. Take it slowly, adding items as they empty or need replacing. You could even focus on just one area at a time; for example, I started with my fridge. You could start with your pantry or bathroom cupboard.

A: plastic to replace	B: alternative option
toothbrush	bamboo toothbrush, purchased online or at a health food store – can be composted or reused in the garden
popcorn packet	buy from bulk store in your own cloth bag or jar
tissue packet	cloth hankies – second-hand stores have a lot
tampons	menstrual cup or cloth pads
shampoo and conditioner bottles	shampoo and conditioner bar, or buy in bulk using your own bottles from a bulk store
shaving razor	stainless steel safety razor – blades are replaceable and can be bought wrapped in cardboard
hummus container	make your own or buy from deli using your own container

There are now programs to recycle soft plastics. If you have access to one, make sure you have a separate bin for them.
If you're moving food scraps to a different bin, your 'rubbish' bin can be lined with newspaper – and you might eventually look at downsizing it!
Check with your local council that you're putting the right things into your recycling bin.
Food scraps can sometimes be put in a green bin or composted.

THE TALK

If you have a family or live with others, it's worthwhile sitting down to have a chat about the changes you want to make. The bin audit is a great way to engage people in the issues around waste. But no-one likes to be forced into doing anything, so I encourage gentle invitation through conversation and leading by example, plus buckets of patience. It could go something like this:

'I heard the other day the average Australian family produces enough rubbish to fill a three-bedroom house. I wouldn't mind cutting back so the next generation doesn't have to deal with all this rubbish. I've been looking at what I'm throwing in the bin, and it turns out there's a lot of food scraps, which can be composted. Would you like to start helping me do this?'

The emphasis is on *I*. Pointing out what others are throwing away might lead to arguments, as if you're singling them out as uncaring individuals. The question at the end casually invites them to join you. Don't feel abandoned if no-one jumps on board yet; it might take some time and that's okay.

If you find members of your household starting to get inquisitive, keep the conversations going. They don't have to take place around the dinner table either. Take a walk at the park or beach. Point out any rubbish and ask questions: Where does our waste come from? Where does it go? How could this rubbish impact on the environment? They may not have an answer, but you have planted a seed of thought and who knows how or when it will sprout.

When I moved in with The Builder he knew about my plastic-free lifestyle and supported it, but he didn't comprehend why I chose to avoid plastic completely. I invited him to watch the movie *Bag It* with me, promising him it was funny and not depressing (both true!). It really helped him understand why I became this crazy plastic-free lady, and he jumped on board with the journey as well.

When individuals from your household or even friends decide to follow your lead, don't forget to talk about how everyone is feeling. Letting go of some items that come wrapped in plastic can be sad or frustrating. Give space for people to voice their opinions, discuss compromises and find a balance.

Tip

Movies provide an entertaining and informative way of introducing the problems associated with plastic and rubbish to family and friends. After all, a movie was what inspired me on my journey!

BUYING UNPACKAGED

While doing your bin, reycling or plastic audit, you might start to look at your shopping list, wondering how to buy the things you use every day, like food and cleaning products, unpackaged. There are many different ways to find unwrapped alternatives near you. Zero-waste communities on social media as well as apps, websites and even a humble internet search are all goldmines of information for finding something like unpackaged tofu in your area. There are tips throughout this book on how to find your basics, including food, cleaning and beauty products, with minimal packaging. But first, let's look at the main options to help you in your search.

BULK STORES

A bulk store is similar to how we used to shop before everything was prepackaged, and in some parts of the world it's still normal. Food items and other products are transported from the producer or distributor directly to a bulk store in large bags or drums. When the bags and drums arrive at the store, they are either transferred to generic dispensing units or left on the floor of the shop as is. Nothing is sold as 250-gram serves in brightly coloured, unnecessary packaging; instead, shoppers come along with our own cloth bags, glass jars and bottles. These containers are weighed first, by either yourself or by the storekeeper. You can write down the weight of the container and bag on a piece of paper or save it in your phone; some stores use stickers to record these details. Fill your container or bags with what you need from the bulk bins, write down the code or product name and, when you are ready to pay, the storekeeper will deduct the weight of your container or bag – referred to as its *tare* weight – from the total weight.

There has been a growing trend of bulk stores opening around the world; large cities might even have a number of chain or independent bulk stores. These may sell a range of unpackaged dry and wet goods for all areas of your home, from tahini and chocolate, to shampoo and washing powder. If it's your first time shopping in a bulk store, let them know and they'll gladly help you out or point you in the direction of the helpful instructions available. Make sure all containers you bring along have been cleaned.

> **Tip**
>
> Glass jars are one of the most useful containers for bulk shopping. They can be kept from previous purchases, bought at charity stores or garage sales, and even collected from family and friends.

According to the Bulk is Green Council, consumers can save from 10 to 65 per cent by shopping at a bulk store. You are not paying for excess packaging or the process of packing things into individual portions. And a study by the UK's Waste and Resources Action Programme (WRAP) found that bulk shopping offered a 96 per cent environmental saving through the reduction of packaging. Shoppers can dictate how much they need, resulting in less food waste. You might also find that some of the ingredients you buy unpackaged from bulk stores can be used in multiple areas of your home, resulting in less time spent shopping and more money saved. There aren't aisles and aisles of stuff to get lost in with bright lights and shelves crowded with the same products by different brands (often owned by the same company). After a couple of months, the over-packaged supermarket that you used to frequent will be a distant memory.

Storage is very easy, especially if you purchase your items in glass jars. They can be taken from your bags and put straight on the shelf. If you decide to use cloth bags to buy your dry goods, I suggest investing in a funnel to help transfer things from your bags to glass jars, or you risk items like rice going everywhere.

Fact

Plastic bottles and plastic lids are two of the top ten items found on coastal clean-ups.

Tip

An old plastic bottle can be turned into a funnel – just cut the bottle straight in half, or at an angle if you want to be able to use it as a scoop as well (in that case, remember to keep the bottle lid).

CO-OPS

A co-op is similar to a bulk store but, rather than everything being shipped to a bricks-and-mortar shop, the whole operation is run – by volunteers – out of someone's home or a public room. A co-op is a way for people to come together to buy staple items in larger quantities at an affordable price; it is often cheaper than an actual bulk store since there are no wages or rent to pay. Memberships are usually required (generally around $30 per year); meetings are held yearly or half-yearly, with decisions made by the group for the group. It is a great way for rural communities to reduce their packaging when they are not within reach of a physical store.

If you are looking at starting your own co-op, here are some tips.

☐ Find a space to receive and organise the bulk orders. Look into community spaces donated by a council, church or other organisation for free or at a low cost.

☐ Set a time for members of the group to pick up their items, like the first Friday of the month.

☐ Decide on a membership price to cover costs like bins, scoops, scales, stationery and freight, as well as excess stock – otherwise goods could be sold with a slight markup.

☐ Make a roster system for members to work a few times a year helping with food pick-up and packing up.

☐ Elect a committee, including a coordinator, communications assistant, purchase order member, treasurer and stock-take member. Positions should be held for a year at a time.

☐ Create some rules of association and a strategic plan – reach out to another co-op and they will likely be open to help you with this!

WHAT IF I DON'T HAVE A BULK STORE OR CO-OP NEAR ME?

Ethnic food stores, health food stores, greengrocers, food markets and local farmers' markets – even your local butcher, baker or deli – can have options available to buy in bulk; all it takes is stepping inside or calling to find out. You might notice that most of the alternatives for buying unpackaged food come from small businesses. Supporting my local community by choosing a local business is a benefit I've come to love. I enjoy knowing who grew and cooked my food and where it has travelled from.

Some bulk stores also have online stores. Obviously this means that the items will still need to be packaged to be sent to you, but most online bulk stores offer eco-friendly recyclable, compostable or reusable packaging.

Even if you only have access to a normal supermarket or shopping centre, there are still things that you can do to reduce packaging.

☐ Choose what you can unpackaged and don't forget to take some reusable cloth produce bags to use instead of the plastic ones.

☐ Look for glass, tin and cardboard packaging that will recycle easily – for instance, cardboard packets with plastic windows need to be separated properly before recycling.

☐ Opt to buy the largest container of each if possible, meaning there will be less packaging created.

☐ Look at supporting locally made products that won't have travelled so far to get to you, therefore using less fossil fuels.

☐ Check on local zero-waste Facebook groups for suggestions on which brands have no sneaky plastics hiding inside the packaging.

☐ This is also a good time to question whether you really need that item: could it be made from scratch or could you find a substitute?

Tip

When buying anything online, email or call the company to check how everything will be packed and packaged, and request no or mimimal plastic.

TIPS ON USING REUSABLES

Reusing bags, jars, bottles and containers will help reduce waste. But it's not the normal choice for many, which is why some businesses might look at you sideways when you walk to the counter clutching your container, a mix of excitement and nerves. I know that's how I felt on my first few attempts, and still do sometimes.

Here is an example of the type of conversation The Builder and I start with when we approach a business for the first time:

'Hello, I'm trying to reduce some of the plastic in my life and shop how our great-grandparents used too. Can I have the loaf of bread/200 grams of cheddar cheese in my bag/container please?'

Time your visits for when the store is less busy; this will give you and the server a chance to have a quick chat about what you are hoping to achieve. But there is no need to go into the details on the plight of plastic pollution, as it can be polarising for many people and they just might not have enough time to digest it all. After all, they are at work. I also don't want to point a finger at them or shame them.

Remember that your server is likely new to this too and some patience may be required. They may never have had to use the tare method on their scales, let alone fill a customer's container brought from home. Make sure to watch them during the process during the early days, as they could reach for plastic out of habit. You might have to repeat your request during the first handful of visits, but eventually they will see you walk in, take the container and complete the transaction with perfect ease. Once you've had a few months of getting to know one another, then you could start to chat about why you're using less plastic.

If you are ever refused the use of your container, don't get disheartened. Sometimes there is confusion with the server as to whether they are breaching health and safety codes, and they will automatically say no to be safe. Remind yourself that the server just might not have awareness about the issue yet. I also suggest checking your local food-handling laws first so that you can make your requests with confidence.

Fact

Under the *Food Act* and Australia New Zealand Code, it is the responsibility of a food business to produce safe and suitable food. Neither references packaging that is provided by the customer, meaning this is up to individual businesses.

Cloth bags are good for carrying groceries home, buying bread from the baker or collecting fruit and vegetables without the plastic produce bags.

WHAT I TAKE SHOPPING

Glass containers (with reusable plastic lids) are so handy because you can collect ingredients in them, cook in them and then transfer them straight to the fridge to store the leftovers.

I use glass jars for a million things – to collect food and cleaning products from bulk stores, to store my leftovers or beauty products, to fill with treats for gifts – and they can be reused over and over!

I kept all my old plastic containers since so many resources and energy went into making them. (Try not to keep hot foods in the plastic too long as heat causes chemicals to leach into food more quickly.)

Glass bottles have all the same uses as jars, plus you can also use them for home-made lemonade (page 176), or wine and beer refills.

SO I DON'T HAVE TO MAKE EVERYTHING FROM SCRATCH?

Some people enjoy the self-reliance a zero-waste lifestyle brings them, relishing in making everything from scratch. Sometimes it's easier to make a lot of foods and products at home because there is not a zero-waste version available yet. But I'm no full-time do-it-yourself guru and you don't have to be either. I'm aware that the time, ingredients, materials or even the drive required to do it all yourself is not for everyone. Human beings have sought the services of others for hundreds of years – bakeries have been around since the Roman times!

It's also a disservice if we feel we're the only ones who have to make changes. Businesses can and should make changes to reduce their rubbish; they have as much responsibility as anyone. It's also great to support businesses that are offering alternatives where you can. So if you start making your own products from scratch then later find it's not working for you, you haven't 'failed' at zero-waste living. Remember, living zero waste within a linear system can be hard. Trying to do it all perfectly can lead to eco-burnout.

There are three other practices that will pop up frequently over the next chapters. Participating in each one is another step to creating a circular economy.

☐ sharing and borrowing

☐ repairing

☐ choosing second-hand

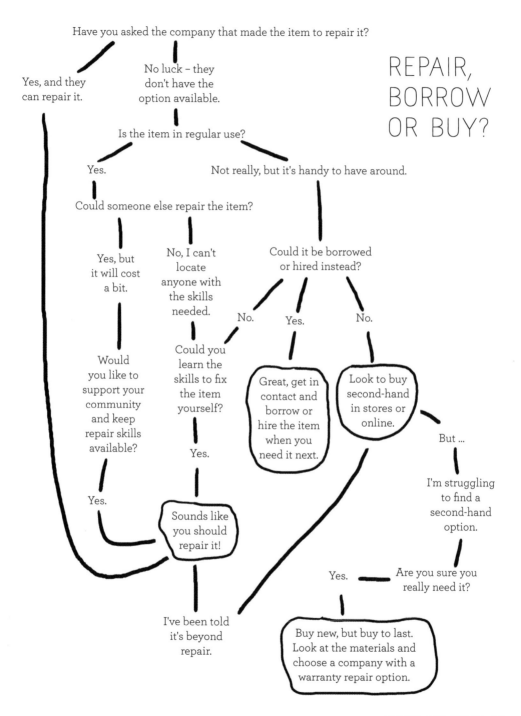

Have you asked the company that made the item to repair it?

Yes, and they can repair it.

No luck – they don't have the option available.

REPAIR, BORROW OR BUY?

Is the item in regular use?

Yes.

Not really, but it's handy to have around.

Could someone else repair the item?

Yes, but it will cost a bit.

No, I can't locate anyone with the skills needed.

Could it be borrowed or hired instead?

No.

Yes.

No.

Would you like to support your community and keep repair skills available?

Could you learn the skills to fix the item yourself?

Great, get in contact and borrow or hire the item when you need it next.

Look to buy second-hand in stores or online.

But ...

Yes.

Yes.

I'm struggling to find a second-hand option.

Sounds like you should repair it!

Yes.

Are you sure you really need it?

I've been told it's beyond repair.

Buy new, but buy to last. Look at the materials and choose a company with a warranty repair option.

SHARING + BORROWING

Three years ago my blender broke. It was the middle of winter and I had planned to make a creamy pumpkin soup for the week. The idea of mashing the pumpkin through a sieve crossed my mind but was quickly overtaken with the need to buy a new blender – everyone has a blender. I started looking at blenders online and announced to The Builder I was going to buy one, listing everything I'd use it for.

His response?

'Why don't you borrow a blender from one of my sisters – that way you'll know if it's something you really need. After all, do you really need a blender, or do you only need to blend?'

I was left dumbstruck by this obvious solution. Messages were sent out, and within an hour I had a blender in my hand. It was used, cleaned, packed back up and returned to its owner, while I was left with delicious soup. Not only did I save resources, I also saved money and space in my kitchen cupboard, plus I opened up a relationship where I now share things freely with the person who lent me their kitchen appliance.

So do you need a blender, or do you only need to blend?

The sharing economy, also known as *collaborative consumption*, is all about sharing items with our neighbours. Sharing is a key pillar of not only zero-waste living but also sustainability and community engagement. Sharing and borrowing promotes trust and encourages people to look after the stuff they are lending out or borrowing themselves. I believe we can consciously consume our way to a low-waste lifestyle if we change the narrative on how we bring material possessions into our lives through sharing and borrowing. You'll be surprised by how much you can source just from friends and family, but otherwise there are a number of other resources open to us, including libraries (not just for books and DVDs – there are also toy and tool libraries) or online communities.

REPAIRING

What happened to the broken blender I mentioned before? I saved it from landfill by having it repaired. Once upon a time, many moons ago, this blender would have gone into the bin, or I would have done something sneaky and dropped said item into a charity bin expecting someone to fix it. I didn't realise that this was an unfair expectation, that charity stores don't have the services, time or money to fix our stuff. These days, I have my broken items fixed, from electrical goods to shoes to clothes and everything in between.

I did meet some mental resistance when fixing the blender. It had originally cost me $20 from a large discount chain. To get it repaired was going to cost me $30. What I thought was a bargain at the time turned out to be a bargain only for me (and a pretty short-term bargain at that). There were many people not paid fairly along the way so that I could buy a kitchen gadget for $20. I often wonder what the people who put our products together would think if they knew that many of those products are designed with planned obsolescence so that we are kept in the cycle of buying new. It is disrespectful to their hours, energy and skills for us to throw stuff out that can be repaired. Yes, repairing my blender cost me more than buying a new one, but it offered a small piece of validation to the person who spent their time making it. Repairing is as much about respect as it is about keeping our stuff out of landfill and saving resources. And if we don't ask, companies won't make products that can be repaired.

CHOOSING SECOND-HAND

I think we could all agree there is too much stuff in the world, even just by looking in our own homes. Walking along any busy street you'll see stores filled with more stuff – even our second-hand stores are filled to the brim with perfectly good wares. If I'm unable to borrow or repair an item, I'll look for the second-hand option. Not only will choosing second-hand keep resources out of landfill and create less waste, choosing second-hand has a positive effect upstream and downstream. By reusing what is already available, you reduce waste and emissions from the production and transport of goods, since second-hand goods rarely travel far, and money often stays within the community. Buying second-hand is a way to vote with your dollar.

WASTE JARS

If you have been browsing zero-waste websites, you may have come across individuals who collect their rubbish in a jar. I think it's a neat idea and a fun way to track what and where rubbish is created. But while some people like to use a waste jar, others don't. You are by no means a failure should yours be bigger than someone else's or if you don't have one at all. They are not there to measure people up against one another, simply to measure your own journey.

For full disclosure, I have a jar of rubbish. It's an old Moccona coffee jar about the size of my head. These days I use it with school kids, who love sorting through the contents and imagining ways to reduce waste. I have had some adults at talks and workshops say to me that they were disappointed and thought it would be smaller. I don't mind, because it's my journey and I'm doing the best I can, and so should you – big jar, small jar or no jar.

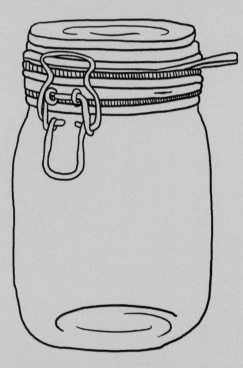

PART TWO

TIPS

KITCHEN
+ FOOD

Our kitchens are the heart of our homes. They're where we make meals to nourish our bodies and a popular space to entertain family and friends, creating memories along the way. The kitchen is the one room updated each week as we fill cupboards, fruit bowls, fridges and freezers with food. It's also where the most waste is made.

If you completed the bin audit in the previous chapter, the results would have shown that food packaging and scraps are what fill most of our bins. Understanding what I was throwing into my bin and where my rubbish was coming from helped me make changes. By adjusting our habits, the amount in our kitchen bins can easily be reduced.

Consuming only what we need, reducing or removing our reliance on excess packaging, reminding ourselves that humans thrived for a long time without many of the assumed 'convenience' items we now have lining our kitchen shelves are all thing to keep in mind when we shop. It might appear daunting, but you will find yourself more connected to your food, where it came from and the farmers and makers. You could try making some more basic foods from scratch. You might even be inspired to start growing some of your own food at home, assisted by your nutritious home-made compost.

If you don't want to make something from scratch and can't find it in bulk, don't stress. We (the consumers) have somehow been lumped with the obligation to make the right environmental choice, when really it's the big companies that can and should reduce their packaging and provide more sustainable choices. I believe the responsibility works both ways.

> **Tip**
>
> It's not just food that creates waste in the kitchen. Switch paper towels and napkins for tea towels (dish towels) and cloth serviettes. And instead of baking paper and cupcake cases, rub butter or oil on your pans and baking moulds, followed by a dusting of flour – or try a reusable silicone baking sheet.

BUYING FOOD

Getting yourself prepared and finding places to shop low-waste was covered in the last chapter. You might have closed that chapter feeling empowered, ready to begin your journey to less waste. Then you threw open the doors of your pantry and fridge, the shelves full of over-packaged food, and thought, 'How will I do this?' You start by taking it slowly, one item at time. As your food items begin to run out, replace them with a low-waste alternative. And since plastic as a material has the longest lifespan, plastic-packaged food is a good place to start.

My transition away from packaged food, especially frozen food, took a year. My freezer was typically filled with ready-made meals; nothing exciting or bursting with flavour, just available and quick. Over time, as I began to appreciate fresh food and eating with the seasons, my visits to the frozen section of the supermarket eventually stopped, as did my visits to the aisles full of tinned food.

When I now buy ready-made food – like a vegetable pie or stir-fry sauce – I always choose something packaged in cardboard or glass, made in Australia with local ingredients, or I visit our local delicatessen and bakery, where I know who has cooked it. And when I'm up against a hurdle of location, time or money, I ask myself some questions.

☐ Do I really need it?

☐ How can I buy this with the least amount of packaging?

☐ How can the packaging be reused?

☐ Is recycling the packaging worth it?

☐ Can I make it myself?

MAKING SMART DECISIONS ABOUT FOOD

Here is an example of how I answer those questions, using pasta and pasta sauce as an example. Remember, it's about doing the best you can, with what you've got, where you are.

Do I really need it?
Pasta is a simple, quick option for dinner when I'm low on time, which, since having a baby, I always seem to be, so yes!

How can I buy this with the least amount of packaging?
I can get unpackaged, freshly made pasta sauce from a market thirty minutes away. Before I had my baby, this option was easier to choose. I'd take an empty container and have the pasta store fill it up with fresh pasta and sauce. Right now the thought of travelling thirty minutes, getting the baby out of the car and manoeuvring around a packed market for pasta and pasta sauce to then wrangle him back into the car and drive home again is not so appealing. But I can buy pasta sauce in a glass jar and pasta in cardboard from nearby store.

How can the packaging be reused?
If I buy the ready-made sauce in a glass jar or bottle from the store, I can reuse the glass for shopping or storing leftovers. Both the jar and the cardboard could be used for a craft project.

Is recycling the packaging worth it?
Glass and cardboard have a high recycling rate, but while recycling is a great option, we need to remember that it still requires energy and resources. The cardboard could instead be composted.

Can I make it myself?
If I happen to have some extra time, I can buy tomatoes, olive oil, vinegar, garlic, salt, pepper and sugar from bulk stores close to my home. If I make my own pasta sauce (see page 79 for my recipe), I can make extra and freeze it in reused glass jars. Same goes for the pasta itself. This will not only save me money and time in the long run, but it will taste delicious!

DO I REALLY NEED IT?

Before I set out shopping, I plan what I'm going to buy to avoid wasting food. By sitting down and loosely thinking out my meals in advance, I'm able to question if I truly need a particular item.

This is a good time to think about whether something is in season and where it has come from. I never gave much thought to the fact that fruit and vegetables are not available all year round and have to be shipped from various locations. The environmental burden of fossil fuels to transport these foods is huge, and imported fresh fruit and vegetables are commonly sprayed with methyl bromide (another powerful greenhouse gas) to comply with quarantine regulations. The shelf life of fruit and vegetables that need to be stored for so long is artificially extended, which may reduce the levels of nutrients in them, not to mention reducing their flavour. The simple alternative is to support my local farmers. There is no need to transport food across the world so I can have a peach or an avocado out of season.

Fact

Teabags contain plastic! A teabag made of paper splits in hot water, so plastic is added to help the bag hold its shape as the tea steeps. Invest in a teapot or tea strainer and make tea using loose leaves.

Tip

On the topic of hot drinks, swap out the instant coffee pods for a coffee plunger or coffee machine. In 2014, enough single-use coffee pods were thrown away to circle the earth ten times.

HOW CAN I BUY THIS WITH THE LEAST AMOUNT OF PACKAGING?

Here is a quick reminder of the steps I shared in the last chapter to switch to low-waste, package-free options:

- ☐ Collect cloth bags, jars of different sizes, bottles and containers in your reusable shopping bags or a shopping trolley.

- ☐ Locate bulk stores or a co-op in your area. Not all are the same, so note what they have available for reference.

- ☐ Visit local bakeries, butchers, delicatessens, fishmonger's and grocery stores to see what they have available unpackaged. Again, write some notes or take photos for future reference.

- ☐ You can do the same at farmers' markets. Although these can be a bit time-consuming to get to depending on your location, you might find your visit becomes a weekly or monthly ritual.

- ☐ If you're shopping at supermarkets, look for things in simple glass or cardboard packaging, and buy in large quantities to minimise packaging.

Once I started looking, I found there was more food available unpackaged than I realised! But location, time and money can place some low-waste options out of reach. If a bulk store or unpackaged ingredient does not exist within reach of your home, is this your fault? No. Are you expected to move house so that you can make perfect environmental choices? Of course not! Find the options that work for your life.

Fruit and vegetables

There's nothing more frustrating than seeing a banana – which has its own natural packaging – wrapped in plastic! Or six apples wrapped in plastic on a Styrofoam tray – which breaks down so easily into the mobile microplastics that pollute the ocean and can eventually end up in our stomachs. I really just want to eat the apples, not tiny bits of plastic. Independent greengrocers and farmers' markets usually have the least amount of produce wrapped in plastic.

If The Builder and I ever see something at the farmers' market we would like to get but don't want the plastic it's in, we'll ask the seller if they can arrange to bring the item the following week without plastic. It might not always work but at least we've perhaps made them think about using less plastic. Some people recommend that you ask the seller to remove the packaging before you purchase the item, which does send a strong message, but check that they will be able to reuse the packaging. Otherwise, you might actually be able to dispose of it more responsibly at home.

Vegetable and fruit subscription boxes are another great option if you don't have a low-waste place to shop nearby, or if you are short on time to visit a farmers' market. A cardboard box of fresh and often local produce is sent to your house or is available for pick-up from a central location. Boxes can range in size depending on household, with options for only vegetables or fruit.

Bread, pasta and pastry

We use a cotton bag to gather our weekly loaf of bread for toast and bread rolls at lunch. I'll also use pre-owned plastic, stainless-steel and glass containers to collect cupcakes, cakes and other sweet treats.

Pizza dough, fresh pasta or pastry can be bought from your local Italian restaurant or bakery. If you are hesitant about asking, don't be. There is no need to give them a spiel on the plastic waste you are trying to avoid in the supermarket. For example, start just by calling to see if they will sell you a ball of pizza dough; if they ask questions, tell them you'd like to have some fresh dough on hand to make pizzas but don't want to make your own. Be curious and start conversations; you'll never know your options if you don't ask.

Tip

Stock up on preserves at the local farmers' market to give as presents for family and friends – I love receiving jams, chutneys and sauces as gifts. The glass jars can be reused or returned.

Dairy and meat

There are ways to find dairy products free of plastic packaging, but, full disclosure: some are harder to find than others. That's not to say options are not available; they just might not be accessible everywhere, yet!

Milk and yoghurt can be found in glass bottles or jars at farmers' markets, farm doors, health food stores and market stalls – even some supermarkets, but sometimes you'll have to ask for it first. If shoppers keep asking for milk and yoghurt to be packaged and sold in returnable glass (just like it used to be in our grandparents' day) then we might see more of it. The zero-waste groups listed in the Directory (page 261) can help you find a local source.

Butter can be bought in a large slab, usually at markets or specialty stores. Don't fret if you've only got the option of butter wrapped in paper; even though this can sometimes have a plastic lining, it's still better than straight plastic.

Cheese is one of the easiest dairy options to buy with less waste. You can buy a wheel of cheese and divide it between friends, or invest in a smaller wheel for your family; just cut it and store appropriately, according to the cheese. Delis and specialty cheese stores can order in cheese for you, or you can take in your own container to buy cheese cut off the block.

If you eat meat and fish, butchers and fishmongers will also accept containers. It might seem odd at first to waltz up to a counter asking them to use your container instead of their own, but just remember that this behaviour was normal until quite recently. If you don't have a container, try asking for your items to be wrapped in paper.

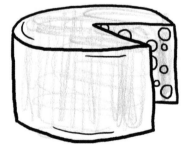

HOW CAN THE PACKAGING BE REUSED?

There are many ways to give packaging a new life, aside from using it to store other items. Get creative!

☐ Butter paper can be reused to line muffin or cake tins.

☐ Cheese wax can be used as a fire starter, as it is typically made of flammable paraffin.

☐ A cardboard milk carton cut in half or turned on its side with a panel removed can become a seedling tray.

☐ Tin cans can become flower pots or pencil holders.

IS RECYCLING THE PACKAGING WORTH IT?

Recycling is an important part of the waste hierarchy and helps in keeping resources from landfill, but, as covered in Part One, recycling has been marketed as the solution to waste, which is just not true. However, with the way our food is often packaged, it can be hard to avoid recycling unless you have access to a really good bulk store. Understanding packaging materials, what they are made of and how they are recycled will help you make better decisions.

Most plastics – plastic food packaging in particular – are down-cycled, meaning they can't be turned into another item. Aluminium tinned food, cardboard and glass jars have a higher recycle rate – but remember that aluminium cans, food tins and milk and juice cartons come lined with a hidden layer of plastic, as do most jar lids. Paper or cardboard packaging can also be composted.

Fact

Glass jars can be recycled indefinitely and will save 74 per cent of the energy it would take to make new glass from raw materials.

RESPONSIBLE DISPOSAL OF PLASTIC

When I started swapping all my packaged food for bulk-bought food and other low-waste options, I also had to phase the packaging out of the kitchen responsibly. Reusing glass jars for shopping and storing leftovers was easy, as was composting any cardboard. But I still had empty plastic packaging accumulating each week. I couldn't think how to reuse it so I held onto it, looking for a way to divert the material from landfill.

Not long after, my local supermarket started accepting soft plastic – including bread, rice and pasta bags, plastic bags and cereal box liners, to name a few – for recycling through a program called REDcycle. Some council kerbside recycling schemes have also started taking soft plastics. Remember: plastic is down-cycled, meaning it is only recycled once before the end of its life. Recycling soft plastics is simply delaying them from going to landfill.

Soft plastic recycling is not available to everyone. Don't feel guilty if you're unable to dispose of it appropriately; it's not your fault. During this transition process, you have gained knowledge on recycling and what actually happens when we throw our garbage 'away', and this will help you make more informed decisions in the future.

CAN I MAKE IT MYSELF?

It's totally okay if the thought of making your own pasta or pastry from scratch does not fill you with joy. Living a low-waste life does not mean you need to become a cook extraordinaire and perhaps your lifestyle doesn't allow the time.

But if you do have time or fancy learning some new culinary skills, along with gaining the sense of self-reliance that comes from doing things yourself, try making some basic foods from scratch. Making mustard, mayonnaise, pasta sauce, dips, crackers and biscuits are some fun, achievable activities the whole household can get involved in. You might discover a love for canning, preserving and pickling. Home-cooked food also makes great gifts.

Dairy

Since dairy can be harder to find without plastic packaging, I've learned to make tasty substitutes with ingredients that I can buy unpackaged from bulk stores or in cardboard from supermarkets.

Oat milk and cashew milk are the easiest plant-based milks to make. Just blend a cup of oats or cashews (the latter soaked in water for about four hours) with 750 ml (25$^1/_2$ fl oz/3 cups) water. Strain over a cloth or a specialty nut milk bag into a bowl, then pour the strained liquid into a bottle. It will keep in the refrigerator for a week.

Many nuts make lovely plant-based 'cheeses' too, and sunflower seeds (also available in bulk) can be turned into a butter-like spread.

Making yoghurt is surprisingly easy, with only two ingredients needed: milk and … yoghurt. The live cultures from the yoghurt are the magic ingredient – I just take some yoghurt from my last jar when we're getting low. Typically 125 g (4$^1/_2$ oz) yoghurt will turn 2 litres (68 fl oz/ 8 cups) of milk into a new batch of creamy yoghurt within four hours or overnight, depending on how set you like your yoghurt. My father-in-law uses a pot and stovetop to make his; there are also many yoghurt-makers available. Try borrowing or hiring one first to see if you enjoy making yoghurt. If you do decide to buy a yoghurt-maker, check online for second-hand sales.

Tip

I buy beans and lentils in bulk and find cooking them on the stove more affordable; as an added bonus, they also taste far nicer than tinned ones! We always make enough to freeze for later use too.

Tip

I like to use the leftovers from straining nut milks as a crumble on top of desserts, or they can just be added to the compost.

MAYONNAISE

2 large eggs (room temperature)
2 teaspoons freshly squeezed lemon juice or vinegar
250 ml (8½ fl oz/1 cup) oil (light olive oil, sunflower oil, grapeseed oil)
1 teaspoon mustard powder

Separate the egg yolks from the egg whites. Save the egg whites for another dish (or the lemon exfoliant on page 159), or freeze in a glass jar for later use.

Add the lemon juice or vinegar to the egg yolks and begin whisking.

Slowly whisk in the oil in a steady stream. By the time all the oil has been added, approximately 5 minutes, the mixture should be thick and creamy.

Add the mustard powder and a pinch of salt, and transfer to a glass jar to store for up to 3 days.

MUSTARD

2 tablespoons whole brown mustard seeds
25 g (1 oz/¼ cup) mustard powder
¾ teaspoon salt
4 teaspoons apple-cider vinegar

Crush the whole mustard seeds in a mortar and pestle.

Mix the crushed seeds with the mustard powder and salt in a bowl.

Add 60 ml (2 fl oz/ ¼ cup) water and the apple-cider vinegar to the mustard mix and stir to combine.

Cover the bowl with beeswax wrap or a plate and let the mixture sit at room temperature for 2 days.

Once the 2 days has passed, stir the mustard, which should now be thick.

Transfer the mustard to a sterilised jar (see page 98) and store for up to 4 months in the refrigerator.

PASTA SAUCE

2 kg (4 lb 6 oz) tomatoes, halved
125 ml (4 fl oz/½ cup) olive oil
100 ml (3½ fl oz) balsamic vinegar
1 garlic clove, finely chopped

Preheat oven to 200°C (400°F).

Coat the tomatoes with olive oil, balsamic vinegar and garlic in a baking dish.

Arrange the tomatoes cut side facing up and season with salt, pepper and a sprinkling of sugar.

Bake for 1 hour, then leave to cool.

Mash the cooled tomatoes, or purée using a blender. If you prefer your sauce smooth, pass through a sieve.

Pour the sauce into sterilised jars (see page 98) for use or to freeze.

MY PANTRY

Look for unpackaged chocolate and other treats in old-fashioned sweet shops or make your own

Sugar, flour, oil and vinegar are great for cooking, and also for making cleaning and beauty products.

Rice, lentils and beans can be bought either unpackaged or in large bags from a variety of stores.

Popcorn makes a good substitute for chips, especially if you season it with different flavours.

SABRINA FRASER BURKE

Coordinator of Minimal Waste Central Queensland

We live in a small coastal town in Central Queensland, a region not known for being environmentally friendly. Mining coal and shipping it overseas is CQ's biggest income earner, and our major city, Rockhampton, is affectionately known as 'the Beef Capital'. The road between our town and Rockhampton is densely littered with cans, bottles and takeaway cups tossed out of cars.

Perhaps the seed of zero-waste living was sown in my brain during a trip to Thailand in 2015, where we saw pristine beaches awash with rubbish, or during travels in Mozambique, where I saw city drains absolutely choked with plastic bags and Coke bottles. In 2016, I asked my new husband, Patrick, what he thought of attempting Plastic Free July as soon as we returned from our June honeymoon. His main concern was going without meat or milk in plastic bottles. I held the idea that we had a pretty low-waste lifestyle, and, compared to the average Australian couple, we did. But Plastic Free July was a rude awakening!

Being a rather quiet person who doesn't like to attract unnecessary attention to herself, the hardest part for me about going plastic-free was mustering the courage to ask store assistants if I could get items in my own containers. 'I'm doing Plastic Free July'

became my standard excuse, at least for that month! Another difficulty was milk for our coffee: my husband found milk powder in recyclable tins, but now we both drink our coffee black and the tinned milk sits in the pantry for surprise visitors.

After deciding to continue my plastic-free journey, I created a Facebook group called Minimal Waste Central Queensland. I began giving talks and published a community booklet to help local households shop unpackaged around Central Queensland. Zero-waste living is still a little hard to achieve in our neck of the woods, so I encourage people to minimise waste as much as they can, without becoming social hermits and hampering their enjoyment of life.

TIPS FOR PEOPLE LIVING FAR FROM TOWNS

- [ ] Start a local produce swap or co-op (see page 53 for some tips on this).

- [ ] Browse online bulk stores and have items mailed in paper bags direct from the farm or mill.

- [ ] If your nearest bulk store is within driving distance, do a monthly or bi-monthly bulk buy. Keep a running list of what you need to purchase and have all reusable bags and containers cleaned, dried and ready to stock up.

- [ ] Find a supermarket 'pick & weigh' (although they aren't necessarily organic items and have some dubious ingredients).

- [ ] Ask your local butcher or deli about how they can give you their products without any plastic waste (including barrier bags and disposable gloves). This will make them think of a solution that suits their business. If successful, publicise their efforts to help others trying to reduce waste.

- [ ] Investigate your local council's by-laws on shops using clean BYO (bring-your-own) containers, so that if a shop assistant says that they can't help you due to food safety laws, you can gently give them the facts. Even better, leave a (recycled paper) print-out with them so that they can pass it on to the manager.

- [ ] If you don't have rubbish collection, start a compost bin near your back door for convenience; you don't even have to use the compost, but it saves you paying to dispose of it at your waste-transfer station.

- [ ] Please don't burn plastic on your rural property. If possible, wash, dry and save your unavoidable soft and scrunch-able plastics to deposit at the nearest REDcycle bins when you do your next shopping trip. Or try to find alternatives to this packaging.

TAKEAWAY

The kitchen (at least in my house) is not solely used for cooking food but also for unboxing or unwrapping the odd takeaway meal here and there. Before I started reducing my waste, takeaway was a regular occurrence. I'd scoff my food without any thought as to how it was made or where the ingredients came from or who cooked it for me – which is usually par for the course for most of us, used to the convenience of prepackaged and factory-made food.

As The Builder and I moved away from plastic, rather than getting food to take away, we'd often choose to eat in at our favourite restaurants. Making this conscious decision was a practice of slowing down as much as avoiding the plastic takeaway containers.

But we're still prone to a takeaway every now and then (our favourite takeaway cuisines are Indian and Ethiopian). To make it easy, we'll phone ahead to let them know we are wanting to order food and that we'll be supplying our own containers, like stainless-steel tiffins (I know people who use glass containers, or even just pots and pans). One of us will visit the restaurant and hand over the containers when placing the order, and the restaurant will fill them up with food ready for us to take home and devour.

> **Tip**
>
> One word of warning: hot chips don't do well in stainless-steel containers, unless, of course, you plan to eat them quickly. Most shops will wrap them in paper, but my local council does not encourage the recycling of greased paper. Check with yours as each recycling program can be slightly different.

GROWING FOOD

Planting a food garden has so many benefits! Not only will you be able to harvest food without the packaging but you'll also be rewarded with healthier, tastier food. You'll spend less on groceries. You'll only take what is needed and, because you've grown it, you're less likely to waste it. A food garden is sustainable and provides you with a work-out and fresh air. You are also safe in the knowledge of what is being sprayed onto it (no manufactured pesticides or fungicides). And children are more likely to eat vegetables and fruit when they help to grow them.

There is some kind of myth that growing food is for expert gardeners or those with a bounty of space. Growing just a few vegetables at home is something everyone can do. Even in my small courtyard garden, we grow silverbeet (my fave!), lettuce, capsicums (bell peppers), eggplants (aubergines), nasturtium, beans, tomatoes, radish, parsley, coriander (cilantro), sage, oregano and bay leaves. When you are choosing what you will grow, space is not the only thing to consider; what you plant should be decided by what you enjoy eating. There is no point growing food you wouldn't normally consume. For instance, I like spinach and kale but not enough to grow them myself. When we began growing food, we also chose to plant a small quantity so we did not feel overwhelmed.

Vegetables can be grown in the ground, in raised garden beds and in pots with adequate drainage, allowing water to flow so as to not waterlog the roots. A good soil (known as loam soil) for vegetables will generally be crumbly, dark in colour and moist. Many gardeners planting directly into the ground will get the pH levels (acidity levels) of their soil checked, to make sure the balance is right. Soil test-kits are available from garden centres and hardware stores, including information on how to fix any pH problems. Trust me, the staff in these places have a wealth of knowledge and are always keen to help new gardeners. They not only have green thumbs, but green hearts.

> **Tip**
> If you are renting or if your soil is heavy with clay or sand, look into using moveable raised garden beds. These can be purchased at garden centres, or look out for second-hand options online.

Gardens need to be watered, fed and cared for, meaning you'll need to set aside time each week, but don't be scared into thinking a vegetable garden will take up all your time. We found our efforts ended up *saving* time, as we didn't need to visit the local grocer to top up on food; instead we just walked out our back door.

Consistent care of your garden helps reduce the need for longer hours on the weekends. During winter we spend the least amount of time in the garden, thanks to the constant rain, and plant fewer vegetables. We find more time is spent on the garden in summer as we water more frequently, plant seeds and, of course, collect what we have grown from a larger crop.

Here is a look at what I can get done in my garden in a spare thirty minutes, depending on the weather.

 As it warms up, I start to water every few days, especially the plants in pots, as they dry out faster than those in the ground.

☐ If I'm unsure about watering, I'll put my finger into the ground to check the moisture. Damp soil does not need watering, but dry soil needs a drink.

☐ While I'm watering, I check the plants for caterpillars, slugs and other critters that might chomp on my food.

☐ If I see any stray weeds, this is also a good time to pull them out.

Tip

Tool libraries are a handy community resource where you can hire a range of tools to use in the garden. Contact your local council to find one near you.

Vegetables can be grown from seed or purchased as seedlings from a garden centre. Seedling pots can be returned for reuse at some garden centres, or you can keep the containers to sow seeds yourself at home next season. There are also a variety of ways to make seedling pots by reusing materials from around the house. Old newspaper can be folded into a pot using origami or you can invest in a wooden paper-pot maker. Empty toilet rolls and egg cartons also work as seedling pots.

The end of the season, before planting next season's vegetables, is a good time to feed the soil with compost or manure. This puts nutrients back into the soil, replacing what the previous season's plants took out. When adding compost or manure, either place on top of soil and let the worms work the nutrients into the soil for you, or mix with the first 10 cm (4 in) of soil. The key is to not disrupt the soil too much.

Like any new skill, gardening takes time to learn. I encourage the use of a garden diary, where you can write down when and where everything was planted, record first harvests and last harvests, and note what fertiliser you used. Keeping a record allowed me to understand how my garden worked, so I could plan accordingly for the next year.

Fact

Fertiliser and compost can be easily confused. Compost is food for the soil while fertiliser is food for the plants.

Tip

If you have a bountiful harvest of a particular crop, search out a produce swap in your area. These are a great way to learn and share tips with other backyard growers.

Tip

Some plants, like tomatoes, may require staking to encourage the plant to grow up, rather than along the ground. It helps with growth and harvesting and saves on space. To avoid disposable plastic string, cut up an old T-shirt or choose compostable natural material like twine to use for tying to the stake.

GROW FOOD FROM KITCHEN SCRAPS

Another fun and affordable way to grow food is to regrow vegetables from scraps that you would otherwise probably put into your compost bins. It's far easier than growing from seed – not to mention zero waste and completely free. We have spring onions we've been regrowing from scraps for three months in our fridge – they don't even need to be transferred to the garden.

Place the end of a bunch of celery, spring onion (scallion), lettuce, fennel, leek or bok choy (pak choy) – the part usually thrown into compost or saved for scrappy vegetable stock (page 99) – into a container.

Pour in enough water to cover the base of the container.

Keep your 'seedling' on a windowsill or counter in your kitchen – anywhere with good sunlight.

Within 7 days, your plant will begin sprouting new leaves or stalks.

Transfer your new plant to a pot with potting mix or dig a hole in your garden big enough for the plant and cover the base with soil.

Water lightly and add mulch around the base if the weather is warm.

KIRSTY BISHOP-FOX

Permaculture consultant
simplehighlife.com.au

It doesn't matter if you don't have a big garden or even if gardening's not your thing; there are some easy ways to get started on growing fresh, package-free food at home. If you want to turn your entire garden into an edible paradise or aim for self-sufficiency, that's another book in itself, but these brief tips should help to plant the seed (pun intended).

Start by looking at the produce you buy and decide where your waste is highest. Some of the highest on my list were herbs and salad greens, because they often come pre-packed and, particularly with herbs, I would end up throwing half of them out. Strawberries and cherry tomatoes were also high priorities because they usually come in a plastic punnet. This also makes sure you use what you grow!

You can buy your new crops as plants (but you'll have the plastic pot waste), or you might be able to acquire them from someone. Another option for some plants is to produce seeds that you can use for next season's crop: you don't get much more zero-waste than that!

Take the veggie garden favourite, the tomato. There are a few different ways you can manage tomato seeds, some of which can be quite a process, but if your intention is to save seeds for planting next season, then this quick and easy method works well. Cut your tomato in half and scrape out the seeds using a pointed knife (save the flesh for eating). Rub the seeds through a sieve to remove as much of the pulp and gelatinous coating as you can. Spread the seeds thinly on some newspaper or other uncoated paper that was destined for recycling. Let the seeds dry for about a week. Once dried, store the seeds in a used envelope or paper bag, ready for planting.

Parsley is even easier again. If you let it go to seed, it will spread throughout your garden with no effort. But if you want to save the seed, wait until the flowers die back and form seeds, then cover the plant with a paper bag and shake to release the seeds. That's it. You'll have enough seeds in that bag to grow more plants than you'll know what to do with.

Herbs and strawberries can be grown in any free-draining vessel, from used tin cans or small pots on the windowsill, to larger pots on the patio or spaces you may have in the garden. The bigger the pot, the easier to maintain, in terms of watering; smaller pots have their place, but they can dry out quicker. Instead of pots you can use polystyrene boxes from a fruit store – some even come with holes in them, so there is nothing to do except fill them and plant them. Be resourceful and not only will you reduce your waste, but you will save money.

ZERO-WASTE GARDENING

Poke your head into any garden centre and you might wonder how anyone could cut waste with all the plastic-packaged soil, mulch, weed killers and plant pots. There are ways. How long have humans been growing olives without plastic?

☐ Instead of plastic bags of soil, locate a garden centre selling loose soil for collection or home delivery. They'll often deliver by dumping it in front of your house and you'll need to transport it yourself, usually by shovel and wheelbarrow, to your garden.

☐ Home-made potting mix can be made with equal parts soil and compost; add sand for extra drainage. Each of these ingredients is available to purchase loose at garden centres.

☐ Do away with plastic bags of fertilisers by foraging for seaweed at the beach: soak it in a bucket of water for a week, drain and use the water as food for your plants. (Put the remains of the seaweed in your compost.) You can also do the same with weeds, if you're too far from the ocean!

☐ Garden centres will sell compost loose for pick-up – just take your own bags, buckets or trailer. They will also deliver to your home. Another option is to contact local farmers for dried-out horse or chicken poo; return their bags to them after use.

☐ Many transfer stations or tips offer free loose mulch to residents of the local council municipality.

☐ Make a weed killer by dissolving 315 g (11 oz/1 cup) salt in 1 litre (34 fl oz/4 cups) vinegar. Brush it onto weeds carefully as it will also kill other plants.

☐ Keep slugs and snails away from your plants with a 'home-made' insect repellent: by placing a shallow dish of beer near your plants, they'll be attracted to the smell and will seek out the beer instead of your plants.

STORING FOOD

Currently, food coming into our homes is packaged, ready for storage. As foods with less packaging are brought into the kitchen from bulk stores – or even our own gardens – it's time to look at storing food differently. Contrary to what we've been led to believe, our food can be kept fresh without plastic packaging. Glass jars and cloth bags have many, many uses!

Most fruit and vegetables can be kept out of the fridge if you plan to consume them within three days of purchasing. The tip is to keep them out of direct sunlight. Of course, lots of us don't shop every three days. But cut fruit and vegetables store well in glass jars, containers or bowls covered with beeswax wrap. No plastic wrap necessary! Cloth bags are another option to hold vegetables that you store in the crisper. Keeping whole fruit and vegetables will help them retain their moisture and keep them crisper for longer.

Bread will last better when stored in an airtight container, like a bread tin or stainless-steel container. I buy bread, croissants and rolls from a bakery using my cloth bag that I reuse each week. I then store my bread goodies in the same cloth bag in a cupboard away from heat and light. A paper bag would work just as well, so long as it's stored in a cool, dark area of the kitchen. Buying bread unsliced and slicing what you need for each use will also prolong its life. Plastic makes your bread sweat, leading to mould.

Cheese is best stored in cloth or cheese paper and inside a container, preferably in the lower section of the fridge. Wrapping cheese in plastic will not only reduce flavour but also stop it from breathing properly.

> **Fact**
>
> Plastic wrap was invented accidentally in 1933 and was used by the US military to spray on planes to protect them from rusting. After World War II, the company that invented the vehicle wrap decided to find a new market for it; somehow it ended up on top of our food.

BEESWAX WRAP

Long before plastic wrap was invented, one way to keep food fresh was beeswax wrap. Beeswax stiffens material but still keeps it malleable, making it easy to wrap around food and bowls. Unlike plastic wrap, beeswax wrap can be washed, left to airdry and reused. They are easy to make, smell wonderful and save money, and you won't have to worry about it sticking to itself the way plastic wrap does. Check your local markets, health food stores, bulk stores and online for ready-made wraps.

2 pieces baking paper, 40 x 40 cm (16 x 16 in)
1 piece cotton, 30 x 30 cm (12 x 12 in)
70 g (2½ oz/½ cup) grated beeswax

Lay down a tea towel (dish towel) on the ironing board, with one sheet of baking paper on top.

Place the cotton in the middle of the baking paper.

Sprinkle the grated beeswax evenly all over the cotton.

Cover with the second piece of baking paper, then place a second tea towel over that.

Run a hot iron over the top until the wax has melted (around 5 minutes).

Peel back the top tea towel and baking paper layer.

Slowly peel the beeswax-covered cotton off the bottom piece of baking paper.

Drape the beeswax wrap over a drying rack. Let cool for 5 minutes.

To clean, wipe with cool, soapy water.

Over time the wax will start to reduce. Repeat the process above with less wax to extend its life.

Once a beeswax wrap has come to the end of its life, it can simply be put in your compost.

Note

Beeswax wraps cannot be used to store meat.

Keep tomatoes out of the fridge, stored alongside fruit.

Chillies, eggplants (aubergines), onions, garlic, potatoes, pumpkin and sweet potatoes last best when stored on their own in a cool, dry area, away from sunlight; wrap in beeswax wrap or a tea towel (dish towel) if cut.

Cucumbers will last longer out of the fridge in a cool location, but must be kept on their own, away from other fruits and tomatoes.

Keep herbs and leafy greens fresh inside a cloth bag or tea towel in the crisper – remove stems and wash and dry the leaves before storing them to prolong their lives. Basil is the exception; it keeps better when stored in a jar of water.

Mushrooms keep well in cloth produce bags in the fridge.

Cabbage and cauliflower can be stored loose in the crisper and last for up to two weeks; if the head is cut in half, wrap in beeswax wrap or a tea towel.

Keep asparagus, leeks, cut celery and carrots in a glass jar with some water.

Remove the leaves of beetroot, celery and carrots before storing in the crisper, as they suck moisture and make the vegetables go limp. Store the leaves as you would leafy greens.

Store zucchini (courgettes) and squash (very small pumpkins) in the crisper and eat up within five days.

Capsicums (bell peppers) and most greens, such as broccoli, brussels sprouts and green beans, are best stored in a cloth bag inside the crisper and eaten within three days, otherwise they will lose their crunch.

FREEZING FOOD

I freeze anything: leftovers, vegetable stock, cooked beans and lentils for easy-to-make meals, fresh vegetables and fruit, even bread. Glass, stainless steel and old plastic containers are all suitable vessels for freezing food in.

Many people would baulk at freezing food in glass, frightened of the glass cracking. In the past five years, I have not had a single cracked frozen glass container – but I do employ a few tricks.

☐ Food should be cooled before transferring to glass jars, leaving at least a gap the width of two fingers from the top as this allows the contents to expand without breaking the glass.

☐ If I'm storing a liquid like soup or broth, I'll leave the lid off until the liquid has partially frozen; then I screw a lid on.

☐ If I'm defrosting a whole glass jar of cooked food during summer, I like to put the jar in the middle of the fridge in the morning and let it defrost slowly. In winter, I'll put the jar on the counter top.

I freeze portions of fresh vegetables and fruit using two methods.

☐ **Pre-freezing:** Lay the vegetables and fruit, either whole or cut, on a baking tray and put the tray into the freezer. Once the food is frozen, I'll transfer my vegetables or fruit to glass jars. Pre-freezing in individual portions stops the food pieces from sticking to one another in the freezer and makes it easier to remove the exact amount for cooking.

☐ **Aluminium foil:** Just wash the foil between uses and, when it has come to the end of its life, roll it up into a ball the size of your fist and recycle it (as long as it is clean of food). The larger the ball, the more likely it is to be caught by the machines and recycled. If you scrunch up the foil and find it's the size of a marble, keep it and add used foil later on until your ball is larger.

Tip

Freeze bread and bread rolls either in a cloth bag, or cut and placed in plastic containers.

Tip

Freeze excess herbs and olive oil together in ice-cube trays. This method works well in silicone moulds if you have them. Just pop a frozen cube into a dish as it cooks for added flavour. Citrus zest can also be frozen in ice-cube trays for later use.

FOOD WASTE

There is a misconception that the food scraps we put into bins will break down in landfill. But, as we saw in Part One, when food scraps are placed in plastic bags and tossed into landfill, they don't get the oxygen they need to break down. Instead, this oxygen-free space creates the perfect conditions for the production of methane: a greenhouse gas that is eighty-four times more harmful than carbon dioxide. Food scraps also give off the awful sour rotting smell landfill sites are notorious for. Most of the food we toss into landfill can be used more effectively, ultimately reducing our landfill sites while helping to combat greenhouse gas pollution.

The best time to begin reducing food waste is before leaving the house to shop. Sitting down to make a meal plan and writing out the quantity of food needed is a good lesson in buying only what is necessary. Keep in mind what is in season. Another trick is to write a list of what you have sitting in the fridge, fruit bowl and bread bin. Before creating your meal plan or shopping list, look at the list of foods already in the house and find ways to work them into meals.

Tip

Sometimes life doesn't go to plan and we may find ourselves with food that is perfectly good, but won't be eaten for some reason. Check with family and friends if they would like to have it, or donate to charity organisations and refuge shelters. Just call ahead to ask if they accept donations.

Fact

The average household bin is made up of 40 per cent food waste. That's almost half of our bins!

COOKING WITH SCRAPS

The skills, knowledge and common practice of cooking with food scraps were lost with the introduction of ready-made food, but this is how our great-grandparents did things! Cooking with scraps has made me not only a smarter cook but a more creative one.

I like to keep the tops and tails of carrots, onions, celery, tomatos, zucchini (courgettes), fennel, cabbage, pumpkin skins – really any vegetable bits and bobs – in individual glass jars in the freezer. In winter I use them to make vegetable stock; at the end of summer, they make a hearty relish (see opposite).

When I'm using glass jars to store dry goods, I simply wash with hot water and soap between uses, but sterilising jars for home-made foods like relishes, jams, chutneys, pickles and preserves is recommended. Since these types of food are consumed more slowly, making sure the jars are clean allows the contents stay on your shelf longer without the potential of spoiling or mould growing. There are two popular methods for sterilising jars.

☐ **Oven:** Place upright jars and lids on an oven tray and heat the jars and lids in the oven at 110°C (230°F) for 30 minutes. Lids with rubber gaskets can warp slightly using this method.

☐ **Water:** Place a large empty pot on the stove. Stand the jars upright in the bottom of the pot, preferably on top of a wire rack, and arrange the lids around the perimeter. Cover the jars and lids with water and bring to the boil. Boil for 10 minutes. Remove the jars and let them cool on a clean, dry tea towel (dish towel).

> **Tip**
> A softer capsicum (bell pepper) can be hidden in a stir-fry or, my favourite, vegetable tacos.

> **Tip**
> Some jam recipes will list pectin as an ingredient to help set it. Avoid the store-bought packaged pectin and have a go at making your own using lemon pips. There are many tutorials available online.

SCRAPPY VEGETABLE STOCK

This stock can also be used on its own as a broth. My favourite scraps to use are carrot, onion, celery and parsley stalks.

Place roughly 10 cups of vegetable scraps into a pot, along with 2 garlic cloves.

Cover with water and bring to the boil, then reduce the heat and simmer for 1–2 hours.

Strain the liquid and let it cool.

Measure out the vegetable stock and pour into sterilised jars (see opposite). Use within 5 days or freeze.

Write how much each jar holds on it (along with the date of cooking). This will make is easier to know the quantity in each jar for cooking.

SCRAPPY VEGETABLE RELISH

Over summer I keep the tops and tails of in-season vegetables in my freezer and make this relish once I have enough, usually at the start of autumn. Swap out the vegetable scraps for whatever you have.

Makes two 500 ml (17 fl oz/2 cup) jars

250 g (9 oz) zucchini (courgette) scraps
200 g (7 oz) red capsicum (bell pepper) scraps
150 g (5½ oz) onions scraps
150 g (5½ oz) celery scraps
40 g (1½ oz) salt
500 g (1 lb 2 oz) tomato scraps
185 ml (6 fl oz/¾ cup) vinegar
170 g (6 oz) caster (superfine) sugar
2 tablespoons tapioca flour
1½ tablespoons mustard powder
1 tablespoon curry powder

Combine zucchini, celery, capsicum and onion scraps in a bowl, stir in salt, cover and leave to stand overnight. (This will draw water out of the vegetables.)

The next day, drain the fluid from the vegetables and rinse them well under cold water.

Combine the vegetables, chopped tomatoes and vinegar in a large pot.

Bring to the boil, cover and simmer for 10 minutes, or until the vegetables are tender.

Add the sugar to the pot. Stir the mixture over low heat until the sugar has dissolved. Allow to cool.

Blend the tapioca flour with 20 ml (1 fl oz) water. Add to the vegetable mix, along with mustard and curry powder. Bring to the boil, cover and simmer for 5 minutes, stirring occasionally.

Allow to cool, then pour into sterilised jars (see opposite).

Cauliflower leaves are often forgotten, but they can be roasted to make a nice addition to winter salads or to eat as a side dish. Trim off the woody ends of the stems and coat the leaves with oil, salt, pepper and garlic. Place on a baking sheet and roast in a 200°C (400°F) oven for 10–15 minutes or until crisp.

Carrot tops can be blended up with seeds or nuts, garlic, lemon juice, herbs, salt and pepper to make a delicious pesto. Use whatever you have and add olive oil to achieve a desired consistency – keep it thick to use as a dip, or thin to use as a pasta sauce or salad dressing. Store in an airtight glass container in the fridge.

Keep your citrus peel to make scrappy citrus vinegar (page 116) for cleaning your home.

Save overripe fruit to make a simple jam. There are countless recipes in books and on the internet; perhaps even ask for a family member's favourite.

Stale bread can be turned into croutons for salads or breadcrumbs for cooking. Just whiz the bread in the food processer until it has broken down into bite-size croutons (which can then be crisped up in the oven) or fine breadcrumbs. Transfer to glass jars and store in the freezer.

COMPOSTING

When anyone asks me what steps they should take to reduce their own waste, I always encourage composting. When food scraps are composted, they are no longer waste; instead, they become food for the soil. Our food, the normal unprocessed stuff, is designed to break down in soil where all types of insects, bugs and worms will eat it up, helping return nutrients to the soil while improving its quality. Sending food scraps to landfill is a big fat waste. Starting a compost not only cuts down rubbish sent to landfill, it'll help cut down on methane gas, reduce reliance on artificial fertilisers and is another money saver. Composting is a win–win: super easy and closed-loop perfection.

When I moved in with The Builder, I told him about my plans to build a compost using a second-hand metal bin. He looked at me sceptically while handing over his drill set, unsure whom he had let into his home. I got to work putting holes in the bin and placing it up on two bricks. The holes were for air flow, to provide the oxygen to help break down the food and to reduce smell. The Builder watched me layer leaves from the local park into the bin, followed by some sheets of damp newspaper, then kitchen food scraps. On top went the worms and more newspaper. I drew up a big sign of what could and couldn't go into the compost and began diligently checking my new worm friends every day.

As our compost grew, the contents of our bin reduced. We started bringing our food scraps home from work or from dinners when we were out. Pretty soon The Builder was elbowing me out of the way, taking responsibility for everything. Eventually, he wanted a bigger compost, impressed with the rich fertiliser it was producing. So now we have two big compost bins built by the sceptic-turned-proud-composter!

Tip

Some council green waste bins take food scraps, but it is better if you contact them first to double check.

What can go into a compost?

green

- [ ] vegetable and fruit scraps
- [ ] tea leaves and coffee grounds
- [ ] used vegetable cooking oil
- [ ] eggshells
- [ ] vacuum cleaner dust
- [ ] grass cuttings
- [ ] weeds

brown

- [ ] sawdust (not from treated timber)
- [ ] wood ash
- [ ] hair
- [ ] nail clippings
- [ ] newspaper and brown paper
- [ ] fallen leaves
- [ ] small branches and twigs

What can't go into a compost?

- [ ] large amounts of onion and citrus (too much can scare worms away – instead use in a relish or vinegar, such as those on pages 99 and 116)
- [ ] tea bags (these contain hidden plastic; instead empty the leaves into the compost and dispose of the bags in the bin)
- [ ] large amounts of cooking oil (this can inhibit the bacteria from helping break down the compost, slowing everything down; check with your local recycling centre to see if they can help you find a suitable recycling location)
- [ ] meat, fish and dairy (while they will break down, there is the threat of them attracting vermin)
- [ ] glossy paper (just recycle this)
- [ ] large branches (these can be dropped off at a council transfer station or tip, or be picked up for removal)
- [ ] dog and cat poo (use a separate pet-waste composting system)

We keep our kitchen scraps in a plastic cereal container I purchased from our local second-hand shop. It sits on our kitchen bench. When it's full, we take it outside to our compost bin to dispose of the contents and then wash it out with soap and water, ready to start all over again.

A healthy compost will be moist and have little to no smell, with food scraps breaking down over 3–6 months. The key to this is the balance of green and brown. An oversupply of the green stuff (food scraps, grass clippings) will not break down properly. Alternately, too much brown waste (newspaper and brown paper, brown leaves, branches and twigs) slows down the process. Keep the balance between green and brown by adding the same amount of both at the same time.

Turning your compost regularly with a shovel or compost turner (available from hardware stores and garden centres) promotes the circulation of oxygen. This is key to reducing funny smells, too. If your compost becomes too dry, spray lightly with water.

Tip

You can keep food scraps in the freezer between compost drop-offs. This will stop any funky smells in the home.

Tip

Once you start composting, you won't need a plastic bin liner in your household bin. With nothing wet like food scraps going into the bin, plastic bin liners are not necessary. If you would prefer to line the bin with something, try my newspaper DIY (page 45) or reuse a plastic bag by washing it out each week.

Garden composting

There are two styles of garden composting: open (a freestanding pile, open to the elements) or enclosed (with walls and a lid).

Open composts are suited to larger backyards. To create an open compost, simply choose a space in the backyard and begin dumping your green and brown matter on the chosen space.

An enclosed compost can be easily put together using second-hand wood or an old bin with the bottom removed. I've seen enclosed composts made with old bathtubs and an old bedroom door functioning as the lid. Depending on space, anything could be turned into an enclosed compost; other options include using old wine or olive barrels. If you are not keen to make your own, hardware stores and garden centres sell ready-made enclosed compost bins, ranging from stand-alone bins to tumble compost bins, which sit off the ground with a handle to turn the contents. Like an open compost, start your enclosed compost by adding green and brown matter.

If your enclosed compost doesn't have a base and is built or placed directly onto the earth, there is no need to add worms. The little wrigglers will soon make their way to the new compost and help break down organic material. If you have a compost bin with a floor, you'll need to purchase a box of worms from your hardware store.

Worm farms

A worm farm is different from a compost. It can be made of stackable plastic crates or from a variety of other waterproof materials. The worms are like pets and require your food scraps to survive. In return, they'll produce a nutrient-rich fertiliser of worm castings and liquid (known affectionately as worm pee) that, when diluted with water, resembles weak tea and can be poured over plants. Many people with worm farms sell or give away their excess worm tea to avid gardeners, as it is a strong and toxin-free fertiliser.

Ready-made worm farms available from hardware stores and garden centres are small and easy to move about, making them ideal for smaller backyards, apartment balconies and even inside homes. Compared to a compost, worm farms break down food scraps quickly. Worm farms need to be kept out of the sun, as worms like dark, cool, moist environments. They cannot handle meat, fish or dairy scraps, and dislike large amounts of onion and citrus.

> **Tip**
>
> A tumble compost is ideal if you are nervous about attracting vermin.

Other options

If neither of these compost options appeal or would work for your home, don't worry. You could consider one of these alternatives.

A bokashi bin is a small system that can be kept on a kitchen counter or tucked away in a cupboard. Using a special bokashi material resembling bran, which is loaded with helpful bacteria, the bin pickles both cooked and uncooked food, including meat, fish and dairy. After two week your scraps will have fermented and will need to be buried. The bokashi material is an ongoing purchase.

Electric composting is like a regular compost on steroids and can process scraps including cooked and uncooked meat, fish, dairy, citrus and onion within three days (depending on the model) using bacteria and heat: no worms required. Units can be small enough to sit under your kitchen sink and require little energy to run, but can be expensive.

Composta is an Australian-made worm farm and garden in one. Food scraps are placed in the top with the worms. As they eat the food scraps their castings move down and into a pot that has been filled with soil and plants.

You can also locate a compost drop-off by looking up your neighbourhood on ShareWaste.com or calling a local community garden, school or even farmers' markets to see if any of them will take food scraps for their composts. Don't forget to ask family and friends as well.

KITCHEN + FOOD TOP TIPS

CHANGE ONE THING

Buy your weekly loaf of bread in a reusable cloth bag – over a year, changing out one plastic-packaged loaf of bread equals fifty-two less plastic bags!

CHANGE TWO THINGS

Instead of covering your leftovers with plastic wrap, switch to a store-bought or even home-made beeswax wrap. (Otherwise use a reusable container with a lid, or just pop a plate on top of that extra bowl of spaghetti before putting it in the fridge.)

CHANGE THE WORLD

Start composting! We throw away a lot of food scraps: beginning a compost or worm farm could reduce what you send to landfill by 40 per cent. Use your new compost to help grow some herbs and vegetables, preferably ones you'll want to eat often.

CLEANING
+ CARE

Before I began my journey to reducing plastic, the cupboards in my laundry and under my kitchen sink were cluttered with a mass of brightly coloured plastic-bottled cleaning products, mostly filled with unfriendly ingredients. A spray for this room, a liquid for that room, each labelled with advice like 'dangerous if swallowed' or the word 'POISON' in capital letters, with fragrances and vapours that made eyes water.

It turns out we've over-complicated what used to be a very simple process. Human beings kept their homes clean and survived without the chemical overload supplied on many supermarkets shelves. Reducing the toxic chemicals and focusing on simple, tried and tested ingredients with names I can pronounce has made the begrudged chore of cleaning a more rewarding task, and the space below my sink no longer resembles a tomb for plastic bottles and sprays.

This new simplicity means that cleaning has become more about taking time to care and look after my possessions, and that principle of care has carried over. If we place more value on our things, ensuring their longevity while acknowledging the effort that went into making them, then we're less likely to let them become waste. Through this journey, I've learned new skills in repairing and found joy in supporting other skilled individuals. I don't need to declutter so often, because I don't bring so much into my life, and when I do declutter, I do it mindfully. It's time we realised that the stuff we own is special and that we need to treat it with care, with the hope of having it forever or passing it on to someone else who will find it useful.

Fact

On average, individuals spend between three and five hours cleaning per week.

Tip

Since most store-bought cleaning products contain hazardous chemicals, they should be disposed of properly to reduce the risk of them entering the environment. Contact your local council to see if they offer a household chemical clean-out or hazardous waste collection.

SQUEAKY CLEAN?

Tip

I use a bar of soap in a soap cage to wash our dishes.

Many of the ingredients in plastic-encased cleaning products have the potential to cause sore eyes, skin irritation, respiratory problems, ADHD, miscarriage and certain cancers. The hazardous ingredients in household cleaning products fall into three categories: carcinogens, neurotoxins and hormone disruptors. When we use these products continually, we increase the chances of these ingredients building up in our bodies, a process called bioaccumulation. Bioaccumulation also happens when we wash these products down the drain; the ingredients make their way into our environment and waterways. It's hazardous chemicals like these that latch onto microplastics. As we saw in Part One, marine animals consume the microplastics covered in these hazardous chemicals, setting them off on their path through the food chain. Common ingredients in cleaning products, which are often not required to be listed on the packaging, include formaldehyde, naphtha and phthalates – all are known to have ill effects on our health. When we spray or wipe counters with these chemicals, they are also contributing to air pollution in our homes. There's even a scientific theory – the 'hygiene hypothesis' – that all the cleaning we are doing is harming our immune systems by not giving them enough exposure to common germs and bacteria.

Tip

Keep the small ends of your soap bars in a container. Once you build up a supply, you can melt them down with hot water to keep as a liquid soap for cleaning bench tops and even handwashing woollen garments.

BUY OR MAKE?

Every time I make my own cleaning products, I think of all the plastic bottles kept out of landfill and the unfriendly chemicals kept away from my home and body. It might seem like something so trivial, but our actions, even when it comes to choosing our cleaning products, do add up and create meaningful change for generations to come.

But making cleaning products from scratch, like dishwashing powder or laundry powder, is not accessible or appealing to everyone. And this is okay. If driving from store to store looking for low-waste ingredients makes you exhausted and you could buy a low-waste ready-made product that works well and is kind to the environment, then choose the second option. There can be other factors to consider too, like hard water and soft water, which can impact the effectiveness of your cleaning products. Remember: it's about doing the best you can, with what you've got, where you are.

These days, I make a handful of my own cleaning products but we buy dishwashing powder and laundry powder from bulk stores, collecting them in old plastic containers passed on from my mother-in-law. Many cleaning replacements found unpackaged at bulk stores are more affordable than their packaged alternatives. I have filled up old wine bottles with liquids like floor cleaner, window cleaners, liquid soap and wool wash, for example. I then decant into spray bottles if needed; otherwise they stay in the wine bottles, clearly labelled, in our laundry cupboards.

If a bulk store is not an option due to distance, contact your closest store and ask what brands of bulk cleaning products they stock and for the supplier contact numbers so you may order directly – if they'll ship to a store they can likely also ship directly to you, the customer. In Australia, these products typically come in 5 litre (169 fl oz) containers that can be shipped back for reuse by some companies.

Most supermarkets also stock products that are packaged in cardboard without a plastic scoop or liner – and that have the environmental bonus of being free of palm oil, the production of which is often environmentally destructive. A simple tablespoon or small measuring cup will work perfectly well as a scoop – or just keep reusing the last plastic one you had.

Soap nuts

Soap nuts (also known as soap berries) are a raw, fully compostable and money-saving alternative to commercial soaps and detergents, available at most bulk stores. They contain a natural saponin – a chemical that acts like a soap in some ways – in their shell. Soap nuts can be can be used in the washing machine in place of powder or liquid detergent, as a household cleaner and even as a body wash and shampoo.

Horse chestnuts are similar to soap nuts and can be foraged if you live in North America or Europe. They have been used for hundreds of years to wash clothes, but do require a bit more work than soap nuts to get the most out of them.

Fact

According to WWF Australia, palm oil is found in half of all packaged products, and is usually labelled just as 'vegetable oil' on the ingredients.

Vinegar and soap

The two easiest all-purpose products that I make all the time use my favourite cleaning products: vinegar and soap.

☐ **Vinegar cleaner:** I always keep a spray bottle of this mix ready to chase The Builder with, prodding him to clean off the toothpaste marks he leaves on the mirror! Just mix one part water with one part vinegar or scrappy citrus vinegar (page 116). Apart from toothpaste marks on bathroom mirrors, I use it to wipe down surfaces, stainless-steel appliances, inside the fridge, built-up soap scum, windows – anything needing a good clean. Due to its acidic nature, vinegar should be kept away from stone, marble and granite as it will etch the surface.

☐ **Soap cleaner:** This mixture is the original spray and wipe! Use 1 teaspoon of grated soap to 2 litres (68 fl oz/8 cups) hot water, and perhaps a drop of tea-tree oil. I put it in a spray bottle or leave it in a bucket and clean as normal.

Although soap and vinegar are two of the only products you need for cleaning, they should never be mixed together. Adding soap to vinegar will turn whatever cleaning product you're trying to make useless. The vinegar breaks down the soap to its original oils, leaving you with a white gluggy mess.

Vinegar can be hard to find in anything but plastic. If this is the case, remember that one bottle of vinegar can replace all of your other plastic-bottled cleaners, and that adding water to vinegar won't disrupt its potency and will make it go even further. It is especially effective against grease, bacteria and mould; it can even be used as fabric softener. Its versatility far outweighs that of half of the cleaning aisle at any supermarket.

Tip

I've yet to find a good enough recipe for stain remover that doesn't use borax. Borax can be a skin and eye irritant; it's better to keep its use to a minimum. Vinegar works for most stains but I do like to have a store-bought glass bottle of natural stain remover for those tough-to-handle stains.

Fact

People often confuse detergents with soap. They both work in the same way by disrupting the surface tension to help move dirt away; how they are composed is different. Soap is made of ingredients that will break down in nature. Detergents are mostly manufactured with ammonium and sulfate salts that do not break down easily. When you are choosing detergents, look for brands that are free of phosphates (which cause another set of environmental problems) and labelled biodegradable.

INGREDIENTS FOR MAKING CLEANING PRODUCTS

I keep my home-made cleaners in old spray bottles or jars, ready for use. I held onto old spray nozzles too, as some fit onto glass sauce bottles; elastic bands collected from the farmers' market work as a grip.

The versatility of the humble soap bar – unpackaged or wrapped in paper – is still something to appreciate today. Liquid 'soap' is readily available in bulk too. I like to choose soaps free of palm oil.

Vinegar has 1001 uses. The Builder's favourite is splashing it over his chips, mine is cleaning. You can buy special cleaning vinegar, which is 20 per cent more acidic than the vinegar in our pantries (you should not douse your chips or anything else you want to eat with cleaning vinegar), but there is debate about whether it is actually more effective than regular vinegar.

Tea-tree oil is a natural disinfectant: anti-microbial, antiseptic, antiviral and anti-fungal.

Bicarbonate of soda (baking soda) has gentle alkaline abrasiveness. When it is combined with acidic vinegar, they work together to clean burned pans and built-up food in ovens. Bicarb is a mined material and I use it sparingly.

Clove oil naturally kills mould, pantry moths and silverfish. Not much is needed; just $1/4$ teaspoon oil to 1 litre (34 fl oz/4 cups) water or water–vinegar mixes. Purchase oils in dark glass to ensure longevity (sunlight breaks oils down faster).

Eucalyptus oil is a good anti-microbial disinfectant, removes stubborn labels from jars and can treat stains on clothes. Plus don't forget its ability to clear a stuffy nose!

Lavender oil is an effective insect repellent, and its anti-bacterial properties make it a good toilet cleaner.

SCRAPPY CITRUS VINEGAR

Not only does citrus peel mask vinegar's smell, the oils contain D-limonene, a good chemical, giving an extra boost to the vinegar to really cut through stove-top grease.

Half-fill an empty jar with orange or lemon peel scraps. Top up the jar with vinegar, put the lid on and let it sit in a dark place for 6 weeks. Strain and use.

FLOOR CLEANER

Babies spend all day crawling on the floor and, let's be honest, licking it too (same with our pets). I like to keep my floor clean, while steering away from any hazardous chemical nasties. This recipe is affordable, low-waste and quick to mix up. I love to add a drop of eucalyptus oil, especially in winter to freshen the air when it's too cold to open a window.

Combine 125 ml (4 fl oz/½ cup) vinegar with 4 litres (135 fl oz/16 cups) hot water and 1 drop eucalyptus oil (optional) in a bucket and use as normal.

OVEN CLEANER

When I moved in with The Builder, the oven had not been cleaned since he bought the house – two years earlier. Two years of gunk. I was dubious as to whether this oven cleaner recipe would do anything and it did. Everything lifted off without any trace of the noxious fumes found in commercial cleaners.

Mix 55 g (2 oz/¼ cup) bicarbonate of soda (baking soda) and 1 teaspoon vinegar or scrappy citrus vinegar (left) into a paste and apply to all areas of the oven with a cloth. Let it sit for an hour or overnight. Wipe and rinse well. Leave the door open to air-dry.

AIR FRESHENER

Some very natural odours just aren't pleasant! But we can easily breathe in hazardous chemicals from sprays, taking them into our bodies where they can make their way to our organs. Vinegar neutralises odours without any risk to our health.

Mix ½ teaspoon vinegar with 150 ml (5 fl oz) water, and add a few drops of an essential oil like lavender. Pour into a spray bottle to use.

TOILET CLEANER

I used to clean my toilet with a bleach equivalent and I remember how the fumes hurt to the point where they basically put me off cleaning altogether. Lavender oil is not only helpful for its antibacterial properties, but it also adds a pleasant fragrance.

Sprinkle 110 g (4 oz/½ cup) bicarbonate of soda (baking soda) into the toilet bowl (optional). Spray 250 ml (8½ fl oz/1 cup) cleaning vinegar or scrappy citrus vinegar (left) into the toilet bowl using a spray bottle. Let sit for an hour. Add ¼ teaspoon lavender oil and scrub well. For tough stains, empty the toilet water and pour (8½ fl oz/1 cup) vinegar into the bowl. Let it sit overnight and scrub the next day.

WASHING-MACHINE WASH

I like to clean my washing machine every six months to guarantee it is doing its job well – since The Builder is on building sites all day, a lot of dirt and sawdust goes through our machine! To reduce the risk of mould, I always leave the door and dispenser drawer open between washes. This same recipe can be adapted to dishwashers too; just reduce the amount to fit your dishwasher's dispenser.

Mix 55 g (2 oz/¼ cup) bicarbonate of soda (baking soda) with 60 ml (2 fl oz/¼ cup) water in a bowl or cup, then pour this into the washing machine detergent dispenser. Pour 500 ml (17 fl oz/2 cups) vinegar or scrappy citrus vinegar (left) into the rinse dispenser. Select the machine's shortest hot cycle and let it clean. After the machine has finished washing, I wipe around the door seal and inside the dispenser.

LAUNDRY POWDER

For front-loader washing machines, use half the amount of castile soap for this recipe. Wear gloves when handling washing soda and keep out of reach of children. Washing soda can be hard to find plastic-free or in bulk; some brands sell it in a cardboard box or you can find tutorials online to make your own.

1 bar (approximately 150 g/5½ oz) grated castile soap (be sure to get one free of palm oil)
220 g (8 oz/1 cup) washing soda (sodium carbonate)
220 g (8 oz/1 cup) bicarbonate of soda (baking soda)
160 g (5½ oz/½ cup) salt
100 g (3½ oz/¼ cup) citric acid

Wearing gloves, combine all ingredients in a food processor. Gradually increase to high speed, until the mixture resembles a fine powder. Use 1 tablespoon per small load for top-loaders and ⅓ tablespoon for front loaders.

DISHWASHING POWDER

If you also like using a rinse-aid, vinegar is a good substitute.

300 g (10½ oz/1½ cups) citric acid
330 g (11½ oz/1½ cups) washing soda
110 g (4 oz/½ cup) bicarbonate of soda (baking soda)
160 g (5½ oz/½ cup) sea salt

Mix the ingredients in a bowl by hand, being careful to use gloves when handling the washing soda. Transfer to a container. Use 1 tablespoon per load.

Note

Washing soda and citric acid can work against one another if the balance is not correct. If you need to alter the recipe for any reason, the general rule is 220 g (2 oz/1 cup) washing soda to 100 g (3½ oz/ ¼ cup) citric acid.

CLEANING CLOTHS, BRUSHES + SCRUBBERS

Most mainstream cleaning sponges and cloths are made of synthetics. These will take hundreds of years to break down; worse still, microfibres constantly break off when we use them. These microfibres then make their way down drains, eventually ending up in our waterways. Even the magic microfibre cloths often sold as alternative 'green' cleaning solutions are a hazard for the environment as they are also made of synthetics fibres. Swap the synthetics for natural fibres, which will break down in compost within six months.

☐ Old flour sacks, towels, face washers, cotton shirts, nappy flats and sheets can all be turned into cleaning cloths. Between uses, I place them into a washing machine or boil on the stove-top to keep them clean, like our grandparents did.

☐ Loofahs, which can be bought in supermarkets and pharmacies, are one of nature's own scrubbers. They are a member of the cucumber family and, when dried out, the inside of the fruit provides a fibrous sponge. Cut into quarters, loofahs make handy cleaning tools.

☐ Swap out the plastic-handled and plastic-bristle brushes for natural materials. Redecker is a popular German brand found in most health stores and online.

☐ Scouring pads made from coconut husks and agave are two of my favourites; wheat germ works as a natural scourer too.

☐ If you are a wizard with the knitting needles, try using a coarse fibre like hemp to knit a cleaning sponge.

Tip
Keep your old plastic toothbrush for cleaning! It's great for small items and grout. I'm still using mine, six years on.

Fact
A two-year study by NASA found plants like Boston ferns, peace lillies, spider plants and English ivy absorb toxic chemicals like formaldehyde from indoor air.

HOW WE CLEAN OUR HOME

- ☐ First, it's off to the bathroom where we spray scrappy citrus vinegar (page 116) into the toilet bowl to sit and work its magic.

- ☐ Then it's on to dusting the house; I wipe over everything with a damp cloth and, depending on the surface, spray with vinegar cleaner (page 113). We also dust our plants with a damp cloth (water only) to make sure they can breathe.

- ☐ Windows are wiped over with vinegar cleaner and newspaper.

- ☐ Next, we sweep and vacuum the floors, followed by a mop in the main living areas using floor cleaner (page 116). Since our carpets are made of wool – a natural fibre – we can compost the contents of our vacuum cleaner.

- ☐ Finally, it's back to the bathroom to clean the sink, shower and bathtub with soap cleaner (page 113) and a dash of tea-tree oil. Lastly, the toilet is scrubbed.

- ☐ If I don't wash them immediately, I put the cleaning cloths into a bucket of water with 80 g (¼ cup) salt. Then, once the washing machine is free, I wash them at 60°C (140°F) and air-dry them, ready for use next week.

- ☐ I find cleaning once a week or fortnight makes it easier to deal with dust, dirt and soap scum rather than letting them build up.

DECLUTTERING

Many people use the new year, a new house or a hard-rubbish collection as a reason to clean out unused or unwanted possessions and, in particular, our ever-expanding wardrobes. As you start looking at the waste and rubbish around you, you might end up questioning your past and find that you want to clear stuff away to make room for what's important. But decluttering without thinking about the items won't help reduce waste or teach us to care for our possessions. There is no point removing something only in attempt to live with less stuff if you are going to end up buying it again.

I'm in no way a minimalist – in fact, I have a lot of stuff, but it is all useful to me. There is responsibility and consideration in how I go about bringing an item into my life. When I clear out the unwanted possessions I have accumulated, I am able to realign what I own with what I find necessary.

And rather than mindlessly dump my bags and boxes of unwanted goods on the verge, in bins or at charity stores for them to deal with, I now pass on my possessions differently. I treat them with respect and keep as much out of landfill as possible. This encourages the circular and sharing economy to grow. Resources, energy and time went into making these possessions. Looking after them and giving them a new home also pays respect to the person who made them.

When decluttering, I ask myself some questions about each item to make sure I do it thoughtfully.

☐ Why am I not using it?

☐ Could I fix it?

☐ Could I repurpose it?

☐ Would anyone I know need it?

☐ Could I sell it?

☐ Does a charity store want it?

☐ How can I dispose of it responsibly?

Tip

Don't forget to repurpose old boxes or bags when packing up your possessions to dispose of them, or to move house. If you don't have either, ask a local retail store or supermarket if they have some to spare.

WHY AM I NOT USING IT?

Becoming mindful at the time you purchase something will help you avoid asking yourself this type of question. Trends move so quickly now, and clothing, electronics and homewares are so cheap and easy to buy. We don't even need to leave our homes – with the click of a mouse we can order an item and have it arrive on our doorstep within a day. I will admit to leisurely online shopping from the comfort of my couch or even while at work, being lured in by the constant sale cycles, not thinking too much about where the item came from and who made it, or what I will do with it after I use it once or get bored with the style.

Living a zero-waste lifestyle has left me feeling free, like I've jumped off the treadmill of consumption. I have the power to dictate what I think is needed, not what others – including companies and their advertisements – tell me I need. I've now set up some rules for purchasing that are more aligned with my ethos. I think carefully about when the item will be used, as well as how I could care for and repair the item and, of course, what material it is made from so I can consider its end of life. Mindful shopping helps us stop the loop of constantly needing to declutter our homes.

There is no point removing items in haste unless you're 100 per cent sure it won't be missed; otherwise you'll just end up buying it again. If you're unsure if something is not serving you anymore and should be removed, I encourage storing the item away for a couple of months. If you reach for it during that time or think about it, then it's probably still of some use to you. Getting rid of clutter is different to removing items that are no longer useful or mean something to you.

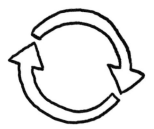

COULD I FIX IT?

Fixing something doesn't mean you necessarily have to do it yourself. You may have handy family members or friends who can repair an item for you, and you can always seek out a professional. Apart from reducing waste, visiting a repairer is an investment in skills worth keeping alive. And if people like you and me don't get our things repaired, our stuff won't be made with repairing in mind. Repair cafes are one place to seek skilled hands. Many new products are now sold without repair manuals, but you might be able to find one online.

Often, our clothes need mending as they wear and tear. Or, if you are like me and forgot to wash a woollen sweater before storing it over summer, you might find that moths have chomped through part of it when you pull it out for winter. I'm not a talented seamstress, but I am an avid mender of clothes. My mother did try her hardest to pass on her sewing skills, but I truly believed I'd never need them. I didn't see the point of being able to darn a sock, sew on a button or fix a hem. How wrong I was – and to this day I wish I'd taken time to learn from my mother, who is a whiz on the sewing machine.

With my mother unfortunately now living in another state, I have found a local tailor to help with difficult repairs. Finding a tailor has not only helped me to extend the life of my clothes; they are also the people to see if I find a great outfit in a second-hand store. One visit to them and they are able to alter anything to fit my shape.

Fact

Repairing provides jobs and keeps skills alive. There used to be more than 120,000 shoe repairers in the US; this number now sits around 7000.

WOULD ANYONE I KNOW NEED IT?

Of course our love for and use of some items wanes. We move house; our style evolves; our children grow out of clothes. You are not always wasting an item by getting rid of it, as someone's trash can be another person's treasure. Think about whether any of your friends or family might benefit from the item. Schools, craft reuse and rescue stores, tool libraries, community groups and community gardens might also be interested. Give them a call and ask.

My favourite way to rehome clothes is partaking in a clothing swap. They are easy to set up, or you could join one that might be run by your local council or another organisation. To host a clothing swap, you'll need a location, which could just be your living room, or an available community space if you're looking at a larger group. Set a limit of a number of items for each person to bring, cleaned and in a suitable condition to swap. If the group is large, designate someone to collect the clothes and inspect they are something someone else would want. At many clothing swaps the clothing is swapped for a button, the button being the currency, to help keep things fair: if someone is bringing only four items, then that person can only swap four items. Items can be hung up and mirrors set up to make it like a shopping event, or everything can just be folded in a pile for people to rummage through.

COULD I SELL IT?

Selling online is an efficient method to move items on – I've listed some of my favourite sites in the Directory (page 256). You'll usually need to set up an account, take photos of your items and write a description for them. Either charge a set price, allow people to make an offer, or offer it for free if you'd just like to see it go to a better home. You could also sell your clothes by visiting a consignment store – or look up online consignments. The traditional garage sale is another option: collaborate with friends and family to organise one or, if you live in Australia, join up with the annual Garage Sale Trail.

COULD I REPURPOSE IT?

If your items are beyond repair or have a stain, then they are not suitable to pass on to a second-hand store and you will likely have a hard time selling them. Repurposing is a creative, resourceful and innovative way of not only keeping our items from being wasted, but also reimagining their usefulness. Before I think to remove anything from my home either to a second-hand store or even into my recycling bin, I like to rethink what it could become either now or in the future. The popular term for repurposing an item is *up-cycling*; it's the practice of giving items more value. While the term is a new one, the practice itself is not; during hard times throughout history we've relied on up-cycling to stretch out the use of an item.

Tip

If you're organising a clothing swap for a small group of friends, turn the event into a party with food and drinks too.

I'm a big believer that everyone is creative enough to rethink the way an item can be used. I've up-cycled an old scarf into an artwork by putting it inside a second-hand frame, the mat-board hiding the frayed worn edges. Shoes beyond repair have been turned into plant pots. An idea might not come straight away, either. Often I'll leave something I know has got more potential sitting in a visible area for me to walk past and ponder over each time, or I'll ask The Builder and other keen up-cyclers in online groups for suggestions. Sometimes the whole item can't be repurposed so I'll salvage what I can. For example, my mum is currently helping me turn the stuffing from old teddy bears I had from childhood into a new teddy bear for my son (okay, she did everything, but I came up with the idea). You might also know of a creative person or organisation who could be interested in up-cycling your possessions.

DOES A CHARITY STORE WANT IT?

Charity stores will take clothes, shoes, kitchenware, furniture, books, small electrical items and other bric-a-brac. Often these are our first port of call when decluttering. After all, a zero-waste lifestyle is the second-hand lifestyle; to many of us, passing our clothing onto a not-for-profit organisation naturally springs to mind. But, in reality, this is not always the best option. I'm not advocating avoiding second-hand stores, instead to be aware of the situation.

Before taking items to a charity store, call them first to see what they need. Just because they are a charity does not mean they want everything. Often, these stores can be inundated with goods and it costs them money to transfer excess to landfill, usually money that could instead be going towards helping others. A large portion of clothing donated doesn't end up on the shop floor; some of it is sent to developing nations, which only suffocates the local textile industry in these countries. Goods should be clean and in working order so they can be sold. When you are deciding what to send to charity stores, make sure it's of good quality and something you would buy.

Tip

To guarantee your donated items stay in good condition, drop them off at the store during opening hours; never leave them at the door, as this is littering. Some charity organisations will even collect goods like clothing or furniture from your home.

HOW CAN I DISPOSE OF IT RESPONSIBLY?

Sometimes there really just isn't another option for repurposing or rehoming your item, but there are still ways you can dispose of it responsibly instead of resorting to landfill.

Contact your local council to see if there is a drop-off location in the municipality for items like mobile phones, batteries, white polystyrene, computers and cables, printer cartridges, fluorescent lights, refrigerators and other white goods, mattresses and paint, to name a few. Some of these items, like mobile phones or mattresses, need to be separated so that parts can be recycled, while others need to be disposed of carefully due to hazardous chemicals.

Call the manufacturer or company of purchase to see if they will take back items or packaging for reuse or recycling. For example, companies such as Dell and Hewlett-Packard take back their own products and others for recycling.

Textiles can be recycled, but if they are synthetic they won't be recycled indefinitely. Depending on the type of fibre, they might be melted down to make a new type of plastic or re-spun to be reused as another garment, but there is likely to still be virgin synthetic material involved in the process. Brands like Patagonia and Uniqlo allow beyond-repair clothes to be dropped off or mailed to their stores for textile recycling. Some charities will collect textiles for recycling; call ahead first and keep these separate from clothing donated for resale, as not all do.

If, in the end, you can't find any other option, don't feel guilty about sending something to landfill. Be happy in the knowledge you'll make choices to invest in high-quality, long-lasting, easy-to-repair electronics, furniture, clothes, shoes and other stuff in the future.

Fact

In 2014, the value of exports of second-hand clothing was more than US$1 billion. The top five exporters of second-hand clothing were the US, the UK, Poland, Canada and Italy (Australia came in eighth position).

ERIN LEWIS-FITZGERALD

erinlewisfitzgerald.com

Whenever I teach someone how to sew on a button, they often stop me to ask (in a whisper) how to thread the needle or knot the thread. So many of us are scared to sew because we don't know the correct methods or won't achieve perfect results instantly. Our fear of imperfection shakes our confidence and can prevent us from trying at all.

I have three decades of clothes-mending experience, and here's my motto: the correct way to mend is *whatever it takes to get the job done*. Don't know how to darn? Try making a patch. Can't sew? Use iron-on adhesives instead. There is no army of finger-wagging nannas waiting to tell you off for using incorrect techniques. In fact, most people will marvel that you brought something back to life. It's like being in primary school, when you could earn a ribbon just for trying. Yay, you – you fixed a thing!

Truly invisible mending is impossible to achieve in many cases and can take years of practice. Sometimes just imagining the time and effort required to mend something invisibly can put me off mending in the first place. Why make it hard on yourself when you don't need to? The good news: visible mending – colourful, creative repair work – is now trendy. (It even has its own hashtag, #visiblemending.) It's easier, more fun,

more forgiving and usually less time-consuming than traditional mending. Instead of restoring your garment, you can make it *better*, adding new designs, colours and a bit of a story.

Visible mending is also a beautiful form of activism. It has a bigger impact on people and the planet than invisible mending because it can start conversations and inspire others to mend their clothes. By proudly wearing a visibly mended garment in public, you're saying 'I chose to mend this' and giving a big flick to fast fashion. All the people you meet who were too scared to mend will get a boost of confidence from your handiwork, and they might even ask you for lessons!

There are many mending methods and tools available, and no one method is better than another – it comes down to personal preference. Getting a worn-out garment back into your wardrobe is the important part. If, one day, you reckon you could do a better repair job, just unpick your work and try again. The garment was broken when you started. You can't get much more broken than broken, so what do you have to lose? You will learn so much just from trying, and trying is what builds confidence (along with a little help from YouTube).

HOW TO CREATE A ZERO-WASTE MENDING KIT

A mending kit is a great way to keep your essentials in one spot, ready for when you need them. You can make yours out of a large, clean jar or box and fill it with bits and pieces as you acquire them. These are three of my favourite sources for mending supplies:

☐ Opportunity shops – or thrift stores – often sell crafty bits: buttons, thread, fabric, elastic, needles and pins. My favourite type of oppy is old-school and a bit 'wild' – you never know what you're going to find. There's probably someone drinking tea behind the counter and a dedicated shelf or basket for sewing notions. If you can't find a sewing section at your local oppy, let the staff know what you're searching for; and they can keep an eye out and set things aside for you.

☐ Family and friends who sew often have more material than they could possibly use in their lifetimes. Sewing produces a lot of scraps (perfect for patching) and crafty types will jump for joy if you can put their scrap heaps to good use. Email your nearest and dearest (or post a call-out on social media) asking for spare needles, thread, fabric scraps, safety pins and whatever else you might need. You could ask for mending lessons, too, if anyone has experience.

☐ Sharing networks (such as the ones listed in the Directory – page 261) are another great resource. Make a request for sewing supplies or lessons and see what comes back. Bonus: you get to meet new people in your community!

WEAR WITH CARE

One category of items that people are most likely to get rid of regularly is clothing. It has even been claimed that, after the oil industry, the fashion industry might be the world's second-greatest source of pollution. Fashion certainly has huge environmental impacts, in the production of its raw materials, in the manufacture and transport of clothes, and even in the ways we care for our clothes and eventually dispose of them.

Fast fashion is the quick turnover of clothes, often mass-produced, by manufacturers or retailers. In Australia, 90 per cent of our clothing is made offshore and shipped here, and we throw away 6000 kilograms of textile waste every *ten minutes*. There is not only the physical waste to think of, but also the time and effort put into growing crops like cotton, the energy spent weaving it into a textile, the hours and skill required to make the clothes and, of course, the fuel consumption when the clothing is transported every step of the way.

According to Wendy Mak, author of *The Capsule Wardrobe*, we only wear 20 per cent of what is in our wardrobes. I'm not suggesting running to your wardrobe and culling everything: capsule or minimalist wardrobes are not for everyone, but you could try it to see how it works for you. Owning fewer clothes does have a practical appeal, but having a larger wardrobe that is worn, loved and cared for is acceptable too. Everyone is different and some of us like to have a variety of choices. Remember the trick of holding onto something before getting rid of it? Before either myself or The Builder move clothes and shoes on from our wardrobe, we'll put them into a box and hold onto them for three months. If we reach for them within that time, we will keep them.

Fact

Worldwide we are consuming 80 billion pieces of clothing each year, a result of our obsession with fast fashion and a disregard for how to care for our clothes.

Tip

Before buying new try renting clothing, especially for big events. There are a number of shops and apps now offering this cost-friendly – and waste-friendly – option.

BUYING CLOTHES

I feel like a rebel zero waster when I say I like shopping for clothes. My love for second-hand shopping was fuelled during my teenage years living in a small town where all the girls shopped at the one store. To find any variety without trekking to the city involved browsing through the local charity stores – or Mum's old clothes from the 1970s and 1980s.

These days, choosing second-hand has gone beyond being a choice of style or low cost; now it's as much about making an ethical decision. By choosing to shop second-hand at a charity store, clothing swap or even local online vintage store, I'm saying no to the excess of synthetic fast fashion, including the drain on resources and the generally unfair working conditions of those who make it. I have dresses and shoes in my wardrobe from the 1950s in perfectly good condition that I wear regularly. With care, there is no reason why any of my wardrobe can't last another fifty years.

In an ideal world we'd all buy second-hand garments made of natural fibres in perfect condition. But I know us humans like to create, and fashion is one of those mediums we like to get creative in. The next best step is to support ethical and sustainable businesses. Look for labels that design and produce locally or ethically using natural or even recycled fibres, and don't be afraid to call or email about their supply chain. If they are proud of the business they run, there won't be much they'll want to hide from you. Choose clothes that will last a long time so you can get as many wears out of them as possible. And always ask yourself before purchasing if you really need it or whether you're just bored – I know I used to shop more when I had spare time.

Fact

Most new clothes are shipped to stores individually wrapped in a plastic bag, and sometimes they even arrive on a plastic coathanger, which is then replaced by a branded in-store hanger.

Fact

Formaldehyde is often used on clothing as a fire retardant, to reduce the chance of mildew, especially during transport, and to reduce creases.

ANAMARIE SHREEVES

Earth Advocate
fortnegrita.com

Your next retail therapy trip can be beneficial for both you and the planet. Instead of taking the conventional approach to your next shopping trip, visit a second-hand store. Fast fashion is notorious for its crimes against the environment. With a second-hand purchase you help to keep a perfectly reusable textile out of landfill, *and* you get to brag about your new (new to you!) purchases.

SOME OF THE REASONS I LOVE SHOPPING SECOND-HAND

Stand out in a crowd. Second-hand stores offer things you could never find at a monotonous store at the mall. Finds at second-hand stores are unique in time and place; you can chance upon a regal Parisian dress from the 1920s. Yes please!

Divert textile waste from landfills. Even with the common knowledge about clothing donation programs, most clothes still end up in landfill.

Save money. The cost of organising used clothes is minimal in comparison to new clothes that go through processes of dying, cutting, sewing, packing, boxing, shipping and so on. This makes second-hand items significantly cheaper.

Oppose cheap labour and dangerous working conditions. Since there are no labour rights to regulate international manufacturing infrastructure, some of our favorite brands practice unfair wages and unsafe conditions in their factories. Buying second-hand means you are not supporting the sweatshop culture.

Keep waterways clean. Synthetic chemicals are used to create dyes that make the colour of our clothes 'pop', but those dyes also pollute natural bodies of water. Buying second-hand means you are not contributing to the synthetic dye demand.

Fulfill an eco act of kindness. Second-hand shopping is an easy step into eco-habits.

If you are inspired to make your first trip to the second-hand store, here are my tips on how to go into the store with confidence and leave with satisfaction.

☐ Go in with intention. Be savvy, not splurgy, by making a list before you go. A list can keep you focused and makes for a fun scavenger hunt.

☐ Bring a friend. Company on a shopping trip can help you in many ways. Your friend can be the voice of reason to keep you from overspending, buying an ugly shirt or losing track of what you are looking for.

☐ Only make perfect purchases. Life is too short to buy an 'okay' blouse. Make a purchase only if it is exactly what you need or want.

☐ Buy only the best. Shop for items made with integrity: long-lasting materials, firmly intact buttons and clothes that won't fray, split or fade.

☐ Shop around. Let's say you had a pair of strappy sandals on your list and you found a pair but they were not quite what you were looking for. Take a look at one or two more stores before making your purchase to be sure you are not cheating yourself.

If you are getting rid of clothes, don't toss them in the bin! There are plenty of alternatives to landfill. Instead, organise your unwanted clothes into four piles.

☐ The 'friends and family' pile should be designated items that you know would be great for a particular person. For example, your little sister mentioned needing slacks for work, or your best friend always told you how much she loved that dress. Offer these items to those people, but also allow them to say 'no thanks' so they aren't accepting items they don't want or need.

☐ Fill the 'great condition' pile with items that have little signs of wear. Take them to be sold at a consignment store, and remember those stores prefer clothes that are on trend or timeless.

☐ Clothes designated with 'fair condition' are sturdy, functional and wearable, but show signs of use. Donate these clothes to a thrift store and also try shelters where people may need them the most.

☐ For the 'unsalvageable' pile, take some time to think of up-cycle projects for each item: cut an old t-shirt into rags, or turn a spandex dress into headbands. How can you turn something old into something new?

WASHING CLOTHES

The majority of the environmental burden caused by fashion happens after we take the clothing home: 82 per cent of the energy a garment will use is in the washing and drying we do each week – and this does not account for the water used in washing our clothes.

Washing machines work by agitation, rubbing clothes against each other and a surface. Over time, the washing weakens the threads in a garment, especially those made of natural fibres. Synthetic fibres are tougher – since they are essentially made of plastic – but they will weaken eventually with frequent washing. All fabrics shed microfibres – unseen by our eyes – during daily wash and wear. Microfibres from garments made of cotton, wool, bamboo, hemp, flax, viscose and modal break down naturally in the environment. The news is not so hot for synthetic fibres. Ecologist Anthony Browne published a study in 2011 documenting the proliferation of synthetic fibres of polyester and acrylic found on beaches all over the world. These synthetic fibres are a type of microplastic. Apart from choosing clothing made of natural fibres to reduce plastic microfibres in the ocean, less frequent washing is another way to cut back the amount of plastic that enters the environment.

When clothes are dry-cleaned, they are submersed in the chemical perchloroethylene (sometimes referred to simply as perc). Perc has been found to leach into groundwater and has been linked to an increased risk of cervical, bladder and oesophageal cancer, reduced fertility and skin, eye and throat irritation. Handwashing or steaming garments is a low-waste, environmentally friendly alternative to commercial dry-cleaning. A growing number of dry-cleaners are opting out of using perchloroethylene and other harsh chemicals. It might take some investigation and phone calls to find one in your area.

Fact

Reusable cloth dry-cleaning bags are available at eco-friendly dry-cleaners or online for purchase – a much smarter choice than the flimsy plastic.

DR HOLLY KAYE-SMITH

Social change strategist and communicator

One way to reduce the laundering burden is to understand that clothes vary in their required washing frequency. Underwear, for example, is a high wash-frequency garment, whereas jeans and jackets are at the low end of the scale. We only need one extra wear out of our clothes to halve our laundering burden, which is significant considering this approach requires no new products or infrastructure. Most clothes put through the wash are not dirty and are laundered out of habit, rather than necessity. Therefore, the most important activity for reducing washing frequency occurs when you get undressed. Ask yourself, 'Is the whole garment dirty enough to be put through the wash, or can I get another wear out of it?' By simply asking this question you will unlock 'bonus wears'. You will find occasions where the garment has no offensive smells or marks and can be put straight back in your wardrobe.

HOW TO REFRESH YOUR CLOTHES WITHOUT PUTTING THEM THROUGH THE WASHING MACHINE

- ☐ Dilute vodka or lemon juice in water and spray onto the armpits of clothes to neutralise smells.

- ☐ Spot-cleaning is a quick and effective method to cheat a wash. After all, why wash the whole thing if only one spot is dirty?

- ☐ Turn your clothes inside out and hang up outside in the sun or in a ventilated space inside (a wardrobe or the back of a chair will suffice for lightly worn-in garments).

- ☐ Shower steam can help lift odours and relax wrinkles.

SHOE POLISH

Looking after our shoes is just as important as our clothes; luckily, my mother taught me the importance of regularly polishing my leather shoes as a way to make them last. This polish can be kept for up to two years.

1 tablespoon grated
 beeswax
5 tablespoons olive oil

Fill the bottom of a double boiler with water (or fill a pot with water and place a glass bowl on top). Heat on a stove-top over low heat.

Combine the beeswax and oil in the top to the top of the double boiler (or the glass bowl), mixing until the beeswax has has melted and both have combined.

Pour the liquid polish into a glass jar.

With a clean cloth, rub the cooled, solidified shoe polish across the shoe in circular motions. Let the shoe polish sit on the shoe for 15 minutes, then wipe off any excess.

If you have a shoe polish brush, move it across the shoe to finish.

TIPS TO EXTEND THE LIFE OF YOUR CLOTHES + ACCESSORIES

- ☐ Handwash your swimsuit in cold water and let it air dry. Lie it flat to help keep the elasticity and stop it from sagging.

- ☐ Try not to rub food or liquids spilt on clothes. Rubbing will push the stain into the material, making it harder to remove; instead blot or dab.

- ☐ Avoid wire and plastic hangers, as they can stretch heavier garments, especially wool and denim; instead, fold or swap to wood hangers. Donate excess hangers to a charity store.

- ☐ Wash and dry clothes thoroughly before storing for long periods, as perspiration can attract moths. Place a sachet of lavender or peppercorns inside a handkerchief in the cupboard to deter any pests.

- ☐ Read the label! If an item is delicate and needs to be handwashed, handwash it.

- ☐ Wash dark-coloured clothes inside out, to prevent the dye from lifting off the fabric.

- ☐ Store your extra soap bars in socks that have lost their mates in your drawers and wardrobe; the soap will help your clothing smell fresh. (This will also help to reduce clutter under the kitchen or bathroom sink.)

- ☐ Keep handbags in old pillow cases to prevent dust build-up.

- ☐ At the first sight of pills (you know, those little balls sitting on your clothes), I used to immediately send the item to the charity store. Instead, use a sweater comb to get rid of pesky pills; the pills can be disposed of in the compost.

- ☐ Keep your shoes lined up and not sitting in a pile to stop scuff marks, to avoid dirt being transferred from one shoe to another and to help the shoes keep their shape.

- ☐ Check the soles of shoes and boots to see if they need to be replaced or repaired, to help them last longer and extend their life for another season.

CLEANING + CARE TOP TIPS

CHANGE ONE THING

Break the habit of washing your clothes so often. When you go to put something in the washing basket, ask yourself if it is actually dirty, or if you're just washing it out of habit.

CHANGE TWO THINGS

Make a batch of scrappy citrus vinegar (page 116) and use it to clean your stove, swapping your plastic cleaning cloths for ones made of natural fibres.

CHANGE THE WORLD

When you next find a rip or a missing button on your jeans or shirt, don't just put the item in the bin – or the charity bin. Look into learning some repair skills or employ someone to repair the item for you.

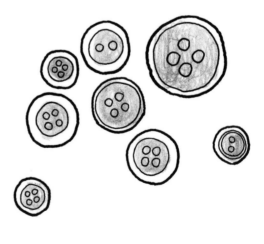

BEAUTY
+ BODY

Face wash, handwash, hair masks, hair gels, hairspray, dry shampoo, foot scrubs, eye creams, lip creams, body moisturiser, face moisturiser, deodorants, concealer, foundation, mascara, eye shadow, eyebrow liner, eyeliner, blush, nail polish – the list of products we slap, slather and rub onto our skin is neverending, and I used to buy every single one without any thought to the wasteful packaging or the ingredients within. Then there are the products that are not simply comestic, such as body washes, toothpastes and shampoos, and those that we use for, ahem, our own waste products, including plastic-wrapped toilet paper, sanitary pads and tampons. While I believe that medicine is one area where we need to use commercially manufactured products, it is also worth considering some low-waste treatments for simple ailments, like the common cold.

There is no hardline rule to say someone who cares for the environment must do without make-up or never indulge in a face mask. I'm not anti make-up; in fact, I love it. I love my bare face as much as I love it with mascara and rouge. Human beings have been wearing make-up for thousands of years for a variety of reasons and should be free to do so for many more. But what shouldn't be allowed is a poorly regulated industry that uses harmful chemicals packaged up in wasteful materials that have an environmental impact that will be felt for generations. I don't believe anyone or anything on this earth should have to suffer so I can have scented toilet paper or ruby-red lipstick in cute packaging. Is my vanity worth more than another human life, the environment or everything else I share this planet with? No, it's not. Being kind is beauty in itself.

Fact

In 2008, the cosmetics industry created over 120 billion units of packaging. Not million – billion. Of these 120 billion units, 48 billion pieces were plastic.

Tip

Ditch the plastic-stemmed cotton buds for ones made of wood, and compost them instead of throwing them into the bin or toilet.

NATURAL BEAUTY?

While I was alarmed to hear of the sheer billions of plastic-packaged units created by the beauty industry, this information was a springboard for me into learning about the overload of unsafe chemicals I was applying to my body. Not only was the plastic encasing my beauty products full of hormone disruptors, it appeared the products were too. According to the Environmental Working Group (EWG), an American not-for-profit, plastic packaging can leach BPA – that old villain – into the products. The BPA does not stay solely in our bodies either, making its way into our ecosystems when we jump in the shower or wash our faces.

I also discovered two groups of ingredients to be lurking in most of my beauty and body products: parabens and phthaltes. It is hard to sort through all the claims and counterclaims online, but the scientific jury is still weighing up the evidence on whether these substances are safe – or not. Parabens are used as preservatives and are proven to mimic oestrogen in the body. Some of the parabens you will find listed as ingredients in beauty products are methylparaben, butylparaben, propylparaben, ethylparaben, isobutylparaben and benzylparaben. Phthalates – usually hidden under the word 'fragrance' or 'parfum' – have the potential to affect male sperm count, the thyroid and the reproductive system. This was enough to push not only myself but The Builder into swiftly removing not only all plastic packaging but also the contents from our lives.

Microbeads are manufactured plastic beads put into face and body wash products – and sometimes even toothpaste – to aid the exfoliation process. As a shopper, you might not know these beads are made of plastic, thinking perhaps they would be natural; after all, rubbing yourself with plastic beads doesn't seem like something anyone would think to do! As the exfoliant is washed off, or as we spit toothpaste down the sink, these beads end up in our local sewer system and, due to their minute size, they escape into lakes, rivers and the ocean, eventually making their way into the food chain. Check the ingredients list and avoid products containing polyethylene, polypropylene and nylon.

Tip

Beat the Microbead is an app that allows customers to scan a product's barcode while shopping to see if it contains microbeads.

BUY OR MAKE?

When I first went zero-waste five years ago, I began trying to make most of my cosmetics as my old ones ran out. I originally chose to DIY so I could avoid the packaging waste; smothering fewer ingredients that we know very little about onto my body was simply a major bonus. But I do still choose to buy some products, especially now there are so many alternatives available at bulk stores, markets and online (check page 258 in the Directory for some of my favourites). Many zero-waste beauty swaps are throwbacks to how most of our make-up was made and packaged before everything became more complicated and pumped out from factories full of synthetic ingredients, preservatives and colours. Here are my rules for buying low-waste beauty and body products.

- ☐ Choose cardboard, metal or glass packaging.

- ☐ Think how or where the packaging will be used. Could a metal tin or glass jar be reused before being recycled?

- ☐ Check the EWG website (ewg.org) for ingredients you are not familiar with.

- ☐ If purchasing online, enquire about how they send their products in the mail and request less plastic.

- ☐ If the goods come with stickers on the packaging, ask if they can leave the sticker off yours.

- ☐ Ask if the containers can be returned for refill.

Throughout this chapter, I've included a number of DIYs, the ingredients for which can be found in most bulk or health food stores. But I'm aware that not all stores will be able to sell you something like beeswax or apple-cider vinegar in your own reusable bags and jars. If there is an ingredient you are interested in purchasing, ask the owner of the store if they could order it in; there may be other people who have requested it. If there are local soap-makers or body-care market stalls in your area, have a chat with the owners to see if they have some of the ingredients you are after and whether you could buy from them. Otherwise check online or post in a local Facebook group for possibilities in your area.

Oil and vinegar are
from the bulk store in old glass bottles.
I buy bamboo toothbrushes and make my own tooth powder.
A bar of soap is by far the easiest swap for reducing waste and plastic in your body-care routine.
I love my home-made chamomile toner.
My cosmetics are home-made or bought in reusable or compostable containers.
I've been using a mooncup since my first Plastic Free July.

THE SIMPLEST SWITCH: SOAP

I used to buy so many different soap-based products, it's a wonder I didn't trip on them getting into the shower: shampoo, face wash, body wash, foot scrub, and then there was the soap I used to wash my hands at the basin. Five different items that can all do the same thing! When I started going plastic-free, I began to question everything I'd assumed was necessary. Five different types of – basically – soap were not necessary. Looking at how much plastic I consumed in my bathroom alone helped set me on the path to question everything, as I saw firsthand that most of what I was using was not needed.

Bars of soap can be bought in paper or without any packaging, can be found and made locally and last longer than your average bottle of liquid body wash. A solid bar of soap is concentrated, whereas liquid body wash contains mostly water. One bar of gentle olive oil soap can eliminate shower gel, face wash, liquid hand wash, shaving gel and shampoo. That's five plastic bottles avoided through one bar of soap.

WASHCLOTHS + SPONGES

There are a number of readily available products that will break down when they come to the end of their use, unlike plastic alternatives.

- ☐ cotton washcloths
- ☐ loofahs (be careful not to purchase synthetic ones)
- ☐ hemp-crocheted cloths
- ☐ wooden and bamboo body brushes
- ☐ natural sponges
- ☐ foot pumice stones

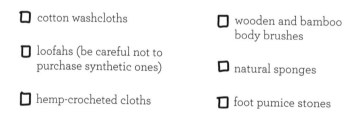

Tip

Hemp fibre is coarser in nature than cotton and is anti-bacterial. The fibre can be knitted or crocheted to make a suitable exfoliating cloth. The fibre will help slough away dead skin cells; when it has no more use, toss it into your compost bin.

DENTAL CARE

Dental health is important, but also a huge creator of waste. Luckily, there are plenty of low-waste options.

BRUSHING

Apart from the American company TerraCycle, which will take used toothbrushes to turn into a plastic raw material, I don't know of any other way to reuse a plastic toothbrush except keeping one to clean grout or to stir non-food mixes in the laundry or garden. Biodegradable bamboo and wooden toothbrushes are one of those simple swaps that will help make a serious impact on your plastic waste. There is a range of brands available; I've found it's cheaper to buy them online directly from companies and keep a packet in the house. The bristles are made of nylon; these can be composted but, unlike the wooden handle, will take up to 100 years to break down. To remove the bristles, use a pair of pliers or soak in hot water to loosen them. I like to keep the bamboo body of the toothbrush to use as a marker in the garden.

When I swapped out my plastic toothbrush for a bamboo one, I also made my first toothpaste, which has been given the tick of approval by a dentist. The same dentist went on to admit that many people can become slack in their brushing routine, believing toothpaste is what removes plaque when it's actually good brushing. I now brush diligently; if I'm at home, I'll brush three times a day. The dentist said he had clients who brush with water only, or with bicarbonate of soda (baking soda) or salt. But this option is not for everyone. Another idea is just to start reducing the amount of toothpaste you are using so you don't go through so many tubes.

Fact

Over 30 million toothbrushes are consumed by Australians per year; they are one of the top ten items found in coastal clean-ups.

Tip

If you are not feeling ready to swap to a wooden toothbrush, try electric or regular brushes where you can swap out the head only. Look for a TerraCycle option in your area to recycle these parts.

CLOVE + SWEET ORANGE TOOTH POWDER

Bicarbonate of soda and clove oil are both ingredients found in commercial toothpaste. Clove oil has been used for hundreds of years for oral health and helping to reduce the pain, and even in some cases the cause, of toothache. I first made this as a paste, but it later became a powder due to Melbourne's up-and-down temperatures (the coconut oil I used solidified in winter). As I mentioned, it's dentist-approved.

5 tablespoons
   bicarbonate of soda
   (baking soda)
5 drops clove oil
10 drops sweet
   orange oil

Combine the bicarbonate of soda, clove oil and sweet orange oil in a jar.

Seal with the lid and shake vigorously.

Note

If you want to make this powder into a toothpaste, add 2–4 tablespoons of coconut oil to the mixture.

FLOSSING

Flossing is an important part of any dental routine. The Builder is an avid fan, routinely flossing every day. I think he would be over the moon if I were to gift him a bag of low-waste floss. Commercial floss packaging is typically plastic, but the string is also made from a synthetic nylon. Kilometres of nylon floss end up in landfill, where it will eventually break down, but there are other options that will break down faster – there are a couple listed in the Directory (page 259). I've also read of people using embroidery cotton, unravelling old silk shirts for the thread, or washing and reusing floss. Another option is an electric Waterpik or a natural miswak stick.

Oil pulling is another low-waste option that has been around for hundreds of years. A tablespoon of sesame oil or coconut oil is swished or 'pulled' between the teeth to remove debris and bacteria, while the anti-bacterial properties in the oil kill the germs. Ideally you would swish the oil around for fifteen or twenty minutes every day, but that is obviously not going to work for everyone – perhaps start gradually with five minutes of oil pulling and work your way up. Once you're done, spit the oil into a jar and pour it into your compost bin. Follow up with a final rinse of warm water. Oil pulling doesn't replace brushing your teeth; rather, it is another step in low-waste dental maintenance. Many people choose oil pulling over a commercial mouthwash. Sesame oil and coconut oil can be found at bulk stores or in glass bottles and jars.

> **Tip**
>
> Keep a jar in the bathroom to collect any silk floss for composting, along with hair and nail clippings.

HAIR

Did you know there is something called a shampoo bar? It's like a bar of soap but for hair. Before I began to even think about my waste, I was a fan of shampoo bars for the simple reason that they were light to use when I travelled and I didn't have to worry about any liquids exploding in my luggage. To use a shampoo bar, simply rub the bar between wet hands, then run your hands through your hair and scrub as you would with a liquid shampoo. A shampoo bar can even be used on your body and face, too. Ask a local soap-maker at a market if they have one without palm oil or try a bulk store or a health food store. Some brands make conditioner bars too.

> **Fact**
>
> Choosing a shampoo and conditioner bar or buying in bulk will save at least twelve (and up to twenty-four, depending on use) shampoo and conditioner bottles from landfill each year.

Liquid shampoo and conditioner can be bought at bulk stores; just take empty bottles. Old shampoo bottles obviously work well, or reuse something like a glass juice bottle. Usually the liquid shampoo and conditioner bought at bulk stores contain fewer chemicals than the supermarket varieties and will have the benefit of being cruelty-free. If you're not using a harsh shampoo, you probably won't even need to use conditioner. I have found rinsing with cold water is all I need to keep my hair healthy, as hot water can remove moisture from the hair. Otherwise, a simple oil rubbed lightly into the ends of your hair will add extra moisture.

> **Tip**
>
> Massaging your scalp for five minutes and then brushing your hair for five minutes every day helps to move the oil away from the scalp and distribute it along the hair rather than letting it build up. While plastic brushes create waste, don't feel you need to toss yours. Use it until the brush has come to the end of its life, then choose a wooden or bamboo hairbrush made of wood with natural, cruelty-free bristles.

A popular movement in the low-waste community is 'no-poo' or no shampoo. Shampoo is replaced with simple ingredients like bicarbonate of soda (baking soda) and apple-cider vinegar, clay, soap nuts, rye flour, eggs, banana, avocado seeds or water. Washing often, especially with liquid shampoo, can encourage your scalp to produce more oil than is needed. Many people who use no-poo often talk about a transition phase as your scalp reprograms its oil production. This phase is usually accompanied by oily hair (how long this lasts depends on the individual). A dry shampoo can help alleviate the problem until the scalp settles back into a new cycle.

Of course, we don't just want to maintain our hair; I've always enjoyed being able to wear my hair in different styles – and sometimes that requires some help. The DIYs over the next few pages will give you some options for managing your hair without the waste.

Fact

Sustainable Salons Australia help hair salons recover up to 95 per cent of salon waste such as chemicals, paper, hair, plastics, razors and tools, diverting it from landfill through different programs. Proceeds from selling materials such as foil goes to OzHarvest, providing meals for the homeless.

Tip

If you have an aloe vera plant, use the aloe vera as a hair treatment. It provides elasticity, helps prevent breakage, cleanses the scalp, conditions the hair – and it makes a nice pot plant!

AVOCADO SEED SHAMPOO EXTENDER

This is a good method if you wish to move to washing your hair with water only.

Grate three dried avocado seeds. Fill a saucepan with 1.5 litres (51 fl oz/6 cups) water. Place the grated seeds into the pot and bring to the boil. Simmer for 30 minutes, or until the mixture reduces by half. Strain the mixture into a bowl. Cool the liquid and pour into a bottle with a small amount of your usual shampoo or grated shampoo bar. Slowly reduce the amount of shampoo added each time.

ROSEMARY TEA HAIR WASH

This is the method I have been using for the past year.

Make a rosemary tea and let it cool. Transfer the tea to a spray bottle and spray over the hair, then massage into the scalp for 5 minutes before rinsing out in the shower.

BICARB + VINEGAR NO-POO

This is a popular method, although a small percentage of people (like me) can find bicarbonate of soda irritating to the skin. Bicarb can also dry out the ends of your hair.

Mix 1 part bicarbonate of soda (baking soda) to 1 part water in a bottle. Mix 1 part apple-cider vinegar to 4 parts water in a separate spray bottle. Apply the bicarb mixture to the roots of wet hair and massage. Rinse hair with water. Spray or pour the watered-down apple-cider vinegar over the hair and let sit for 3 minutes. Rinse out with cold water.

RYE FLOUR NO-POO

Rye flour is full of minerals, vitamins and proteins to help your hair look healthy with a pH that won't hurt your scalp, so it's especially good for sensitive skin.

Combine 3 tablespoons rye flour with water to form a paste. Rub onto the scalp and let sit for 3 minutes. Rinse out thoroughly.

DRY SHAMPOO

A popular dry shampoo brand contains thirteen ingredients, the first one being butane, and costs $14. My safe and simple dry shampoo recipe contains two ingredients and costs less than $3. I can use the tapioca as a face powder, in my eyebrow powder and for cooking: it's low-waste and multipurpose.

Mix together small amounts of tapioca flour (arrowroot and cornflour/cornstarch will also work) and carob powder (cocoa also works) in a small glass jar until you find the correct colour for your hair. Those with lighter hair won't need to add a colour like carob. Sprinkle onto your scalp, concentrating on the front section of the hair. Let it sit for a few minutes, while it soaks up the oil, then brush it out.

DEEP-CLEAN HAIR MASK

Once in a while, I like to indulge in a hair mask, using unpackaged goods from my own pantry and garden. Lemon, apple-cider vinegar and yoghurt help reduce any excess oils. Lemon juice does have the power to bleach hair though, so always dilute it with water.

1 tablespoon lemon juice
1 teaspoon apple-cider vinegar
60 g (2 oz/½ cup) plain yogurt
1 tablespoon honey

Mix the ingredients together with 2 tablespoons water and apply over dry hair, massaging into the scalp. Leave on the hair for 15 minutes, then rinse off.

HYDRATING HAIR MASK

Honey has moisturising properties. Olive oil, avocado and rye flour help make your hair look and feel healthy.

2 tablespoons honey
½ ripe avocado, mashed
1 tablespoon rye flour
2 tablespoons olive oil

Combine the honey, mashed avocado, rye flour and olive oil and mix until smooth. Apply to dry hair and let it sit on the hair for 10 minutes before rinsing off.

HAIRSPRAY

Home-made hairspray is far easier to put together than you might think and uses two very common ingredients: oranges and vodka. You will need a glass spray bottle to keep this in. The vodka helps preserve the spray.

1 large orange, sliced
2 tablespoons vodka

Combine the orange with 500 ml (17 fl oz/2 cups) water in a pot. Bring to the boil. Turn down the heat to medium and simmer until the water has reduced by half.

Remove from the heat and strain the liquid, making sure no large pieces of orange escape as these can clog the spray bottle.

Pour the liquid and vodka into a spray bottle. Shake before each use, and store away from direct sunlight.

HAIR WAX

For something with more hold, this hair wax is ideal. It works well for beards and moustaches (according to The Builder). The wax also makes a multipurpose balm for lips, cuticles, cuts and scrapes.

100 g (3½ oz/¾ cup) grated beeswax
230 g (8 oz/½ cup) shea butter
125 ml (4 fl oz/½ cup) hemp oil
    or jojoba oil
1½ tablespoons tapioca flour or
    arrowroot powder

Fill the bottom of a double boiler with water (or fill a pot with water and place a glass bowl on top). Heat on a stove-top over medium heat. Add the beeswax and shea butter to the top of the double boiler (or the glass bowl), mixing until everything has melted and combined.

In another bowl, stir together the hemp or jojoba oil with the tapioca flour (or arrowroot powder). When combined, add to the melted beeswax and shea butter while over the heat. Stir until everything is combined.

Remove the top of the double boiler (or the glass bowl from the pot). Use hand-held beaters to mix further, until the mixture has a sticky consistency. Scoop into your chosen jar and let cool. Store in a cool, dark place for up to a year.

LINSEED GEL

The little linseeds (flaxseeds) sold at bulk stores can be turned into a styling gel. It can last in the fridge for up two weeks. The antioxidant-rich gel is not only great at holding hair in place, but can also act as a hair mask and face mask too.

Soak 55 g (2 oz/¼ cup) linseeds (flaxseeds) overnight in 250 ml (8½ fl oz/1 cup) water. The next day, tip the seeds and water into a saucepan. Add another 250 ml water and bring to the boil. Reduce the heat to a simmer and stir the mixture slowly for 6–8 minutes, until water becomes a thin gel. Remove from the heat.

Pour into an old stocking, otherwise a sieve or a piece of muslin (cheesecloth) and squeeze the mixture through into a bowl; it should have a gel consistency. Transfer the gel to a sterilised glass jar (see page 98).

Remove the leftover linseeds from the stocking and compost them. Wash the stocking and keep for your next batch of gel.

To use the gel simply take a teaspoon of the mixture, warm it in your hands then apply to the hair.

HAIR REMOVAL

If you are a man or woman who shaves or waxes, rest assured you can continue to do so without creating much waste. After five years I still use my plastic razor to shave, only these days, I keep it out of the shower to stop the blades from rusting. I extend its life by holding the leg of an old pair of jeans with one hand and pulling the razor over the jean fifteen times, then switching directions and repeating.

When your old blade is no longer as sharp as you like, safety razors are a plastic-free alternative to the disposable options. Safety razors are made of metal, with only the double-sided stainless-steel blades needing to be replaced rather than the whole body. It should take between two and three months before a safety razor's blade becomes blunt, if you look after it and keep it away from moisture. New blades can be bought online or at shaving shops, usually packaged in cardboard or paper. To recycle the blades, collect them inside a metal container when placing into your recycling bin or drop them off at a local transfer station. Safety razors require slow and steady practice at the start, as the blades are very sharp. One downside to owning a safety razor is that you may not be able to take it in your carry-on luggage; some countries consider these razors a potential risk. In this instance, keep your old plastic razor for travel.

Electric razors and bikini trimmers are other options to reduce waste, as they can last for years. The Builder and I have one each from before we went zero waste and both have lasted over a decade with care and maintenance. Look online for second-hand options.

The Builder uses a shaving bar on his face. It's similar to a soap and he thinks it helps give a better and closer shave than the usual creams, as you are encouraged to massage the product into the skin rather than slap it on without a thought. Massaging into the skin helps lift the hair follicle allowing the razor to get as close as possible. Shaving soap can be bought in paper, metal tins or glass containers. I use a simple bar of soap to shave my legs and underarms.

Tip

Sugar wax is a traditional Middle Eastern hair removal method using sugar, lemon juice and water. (You can eat it too, obviously before using it for hair removal.) There are many YouTube videos with clear instructions on how to make and use sugar wax.

FACE

My skin is naturally very oily and can clog easily, but that doesn't mean that I need a lot of packaged products to keep it healthy. Most days I now wash my face with water only or do an oil cleanse. Once a week I'll clean my face with my simple soap bar. I've found I have a more even skin tone and get fewer breakouts than I ever did before.

OIL

Someone somewhere has scared many of us into not putting oil onto our faces or bodies. There is a fear of oil causing deadly breakouts with skin resembling an oil slick. The simplicity of one ingredient has been replaced with products containing five, ten or even thirty ingredients. The funny thing is, one of the main ingredients in these formulas is oil, added for its moisturising, anti-inflammatory and naturally nourishing effects.

Oils are the perfect low-waste beauty swap, available at most bulk stores or in glass packaging. Depending on the oil they can be cheaper than most beauty products, plus they last longer, as you don't need to use as much. I switch between hemp and sunflower oil purchased in reusable glass bottles for use on my face and body. You can use oil as a moisturiser and to wash your face.

Fact
There are several recipes online that are suitable for those who want to continue using foaming cleaner, but most seem to call for castile soap, which can contain palm oil.

There are a wide variety of oils available, but choosing the right one does require some knowledge of comedogenic ratings. *Comedogenic* refers to the potential for causing a blockage in pores resulting in blackheads or pimples. Certain oils have a higher chance of causing these problems than others, depending on your skin. For example, I have large pores, so my body releases more sebum (natural oil) onto the skin versus someone with small pores, who would typically have drier skin. Choosing an oil with a lower comedogenic rating means there is greater chance my pores won't get blocked and the natural oils my body creates won't get stuck. When I tried coconut oil, before knowing anything of comedogenic ratings, I couldn't figure out why I was suddenly breaking out in blackheads and inflamed skin when I had read it to be the best oil for everything. Moral of the story: everyone's skin is different.

These are the comedogenic ratings and common oils for each:

- ☐ 0 – **will not clog pores**: argan oil, camellia oil, hemp seed oil, raspberry seed oil, shea butter, sunflower oil

- ☐ 1 – **low**: rosehip oil, castor oil, calendula oil

- ☐ 2 – **moderately low**: almond oil, avocado oil, evening primrose oil, grapeseed oil, jojoba oil, olive oil, peanut oil, sesame oil, tamanu oil

- ☐ 3 – **moderate**: soy bean oil

- ☐ 4 – **fairly high**: cocoa butter, coconut butter, coconut oil, linseed (flaxseed) oil, palm oil

- ☐ 5 – **high**: wheat germ oil

Those with naturally oily skin might like to choose oils that have higher *linoleic* acid and lower *oleic* acid (such as hemp seed, rosehip, evening primrose, grapeseed or seasame oils). Linoleic acid helps break down our natural sebum. When our skin has too little of it, which can be the case for those with oily or acne-prone skin, the sebum becomes stuck. Oils with more oleic acid than linoleic acid will only clog pores more. This would explain why someone with my skin type finds almond oil and argan oil don't work, as these have more oleic acid than linoleic acid. Always choose certified organic oils and avoid those that are genetically modified: these will be labelled as being GMO, or genetically modified organism.

An oil cleanse consists of massaging oil onto your face and wiping off the excess with water. Oil attracts oil. Dirt and other impurities attach themselves to the sebum on our skin; when you use oil to cleanse, the dirty oil on your face comes off with it, leaving clean oil to help retain moisture rather than stripping it away as soap or detergents do. Pour a small amount of oil (sunflower, olive, coconut, almond, hemp; any oil you like) into the palm of your hand and massage into your skin around your face. Soak a washcloth in hot water, wring it out, then wipe over your face until oil is removed. There will be some oil left on the skin. I don't feel I need to add anything else after this but, if you have dry skin, apply a moisturiser, a light lotion or even another oil, if that's what you use.

If oil doesn't appeal to you as a moisturiser, investigate face moisturising bars, which look like a bar of soap. They come wrapped in cardboard or paper and are generally free of nasty ingredients. There are moisturisers and lotions available in glass too, or you can try your hand at making your own creams and body butters with many of the ingredients I've used in this section.

> **Tip**
> When my old face creams and make-up began running out, I held onto the small pots, jars and spray bottles to reuse for my home-made make-up and body care. I also asked friends if they had empty containers for me to use. Otherwise, I suggest looking at local wholesale retailers or visiting online stores.

APPLE CIDER TONER

For someone with larger pores and oily skin, I can vouch for the effectiveness of apple-cider vinegar as a toner. I use it twice a week and see a difference when I don't. The acetic and malic acids of apples help dissolve and remove dead skin cells, and can reduce dark spots and scars. Apple-cider vinegar can be bought in bulk, made at home or bought in glass bottles. Look for brands that have a cloudy appearance, or are labelled raw or organic.

Mix 1 part apple-cider vinegar with 1 part water in a small glass bottle.

Use a piece of cotton cloth to wipe the toner over your face, avoiding the eye area. Let it dry and apply your usual moisturiser or oil.

Store in a cool, dark place for up to a year.

ROSEWATER MIST

If you don't have roses available, try marigolds (also known as calendula), or why not use both together? Marigolds have anti-inflammatory, antibacterial and restorative properties and can be eaten in salads too, plus they require a little less maintenance than a rose bush. I sometimes use dried rose petals from the tea sections of bulk stores as I don't have a rose bush – but many of my neighbours do. When rose season looks to be coming to an end, I ask them if I can have a bowl of petals, making sure to check that they haven't been sprayed with manufactured garden chemicals.

Cover a handful of fresh petals with 250 ml (8½ fl oz/1 cup) hot water (not boiling) in a bowl and cover with a plate. Let it sit until the water has cooled.

Once cool, strain the liquid through a sieve, then transfer into your spray bottle using a funnel.

Add ½ teaspoon of vodka to help preserve for up to a year. Otherwise, store in a cool, dark place and use within 2 weeks.

CHAMOMILE TONER

Chamomile is anti-inflammatory; honey is soothing on the skin, while adding moisture.

250 ml (8½ fl oz/1 cup) warm
    chamomile-flower tea
1 teaspoon honey
5 tablespoons apple-cider vinegar

Combine the ingredients into a bowl and stir until the honey has dissolved. Use a funnel to pour into a small glass bottle.

Use a piece of cotton cloth to wipe the toner over your face, avoiding the eye area. Let dry and apply your usual moisturiser or oil.

Store in a cool, dark place for up to a year.

LEMON EXFOLIANT

We eat a lot of lemon in our house, especially The Builder. Over the years, I've gently reminded him to not compost the lemon he uses but instead to save the leftovers in a jar in the fridge. I will rub these lemon peels over my face once a week, leave it for twenty minutes, then wash off. Lemon contains alpha hydroxy acid and citric acid, both of which work as a gentle peel to remove the top layers of the dead skin cells; if you have broken skin the lemon will irritate. The skins can be turned into scrappy citrus vinegar (page 116) too. I love multipurpose things! If you find lemon on its own too drying, try this home-made lemon exfoliant.

1 teaspoon lemon juice
2 tablespoons brown sugar
1 egg white

Mix the lemon juice, brown sugar and egg white in a bowl.

Rub the mixture over the face using gentle circular movements.

Let it sit for 20 minutes, then wash off.

FACE MASKS + SCRUBS

I like my face masks to double as exfoliants (multipurpose, again!). Some bulk stores sell traditional clay-based powder for using as masks or as an ingredient, but my skin reacts to clay masks with a horrible rash. Here are some others that suit my sensitive skin.

☐ Cool as a cucumber: banish dark circles, get rid of redness and remove puffiness with ice water and cucumbers. Fill a large bowl or basin with ice cubes, cucumber slices and water. Pulling your hair back, dunk your face into the ice bath. Hold your face there for five seconds and repeat twice more. Don't forget to compost the cucumbers.

☐ Honey is said to calm inflammation, improve plumpness, protect from bacterial damage and draw moisture to the skin. Spread a layer of raw honey over clean, dry skin and let it sit on the face for 15–30 minutes, then rinse off with a warm washcloth. Raw honey means it has not been heat treated, which destroys many of its medicinal properties. Most supermarket-bought honey has been heat treated. Raw honey is often sold at farmers' markets and health food stores or bulk stores.

☐ We have all read about sugar not being good for us; some of us who indulge will sometimes see not-so-lovely results in our skin. But when used topically, both white and brown sugar work as a wonderful scrub. Your skin will look so fresh and clean!

☐ Oatmeal is perfect for sensitive skin. It is moisturising and will help with any inflammation your skin might suffer. Mix with honey for a nourishing face mask.

☐ I have a sensitivity to coffee (I know, I know ...) but that does not stop me from 'borrowing' a cup from The Builder's stash to give my body a good scrub. It is too harsh for my face and leaves me looking red, so I use it exclusively below the neck. As caffeine can be absorbed through the skin, it's probably best not to leave it sitting on your body for too long.

SUNSCREEN

Growing up in Australia, closer than anywhere else in the world to the hole in the ozone layer, I've had to take sun care seriously. Being sun smart is drilled into most Australians for good reason, given we have the highest rate of skin cancer. My colouring is pale with freckles; send me outside for ten minutes and I'm bound to come back with sunburn. Routinely, I try to stay out of the sun between 11 am and 2 pm, seeking shaded areas with my sunglasses close at hand. Choosing sun-safe clothing – longer sleeves and a broad-brimmed hat – is a simple swap and works perfectly to screen your skin from the sun, low-waste style.

When I first started reducing my plastic, I swapped to a cardboard-packaged sunscreen with a wax lining, consisting largely of the ingredient zinc. It worked well but I needed something more for the rest of my body when I went to the beach. While there are sunscreens now available in tin and glass too, and recipes for zero-waste sunscreen to make at home, I encourage people to use a sunscreen that is water-resistant and appropriate for them. If that happens to come in plastic, then so be it. Skin cancer is serious. Those twenty minutes after getting out of the water and waiting to dry before putting on sunscreen can be harmful. Choose what you'll use and what you are comfortable with.

Tip

Natural ingredients can cause irritation too. If a rash, stinging or other discomfort develops after you use a natural or home-made product, please stop using it. Everyone's skin is different; treat yours with care.

MAKE-UP

One of the first beauty swaps I made was mascara. I found various online recipes for home-made mascara, containing ingredients I could procure or make easily. One morning I mixed everything together, transferred the concoction to an old lip balm case and snapped off the mascara wand from my old mascara tube. The initial test left me feeling confident and, by the afternoon, I had applied it to my lashes and headed out. My eyelashes are long – if I had to compare them, I'd say they resemble a camel's. When I wear my sunglasses, the lashes hit the lenses, and when I put on my sunglasses on my way out of the door, I found the mascara had smeared onto my lenses within a couple of blinks. I was so used to conventional mascara drying on my lashes that I assumed the recipe I was using would too. Eventually, after a couple of tweaks, I mixed together a cake mascara – based on a recipe from the 1930s – that worked better for my long lashes.

When my son was born, I soon learnt how precious time was and, luckily, discovered more businesses were emerging that sold zero-waste make-up. I now buy a ready-made cake mascara. Cake mascara was the popular choice until the 1960s, when mascara tubes grew in popularity. The mascara mixture is pressed into a tin or cardboard container and is usually sold with a brush. Users wet the brush with water and run it over the dry mixture, then apply to the lashes. After use, the brush is washed and put away until needed again. These days, many cake mascaras are made differently but still use the tin or cardboard packaging, with some businesses offering refills and encouraging buyers to make a purchase without the brush to save on waste.

I'm inspired to see a growing number of new companies around the world starting up with the goal to provide zero-waste beauty products without any of the nasty chemicals we've been fooled into thinking we need. It's also nice to support small businesses with whom I can have direct conversations about packaging and ingredients. In my dream zero-waste plastic-free world, I would love a beauty apothecary where we can drop off our containers to be filled with safe cosmetics rather than continue adding to landfill.

Tip

To remove make-up, use olive oil (or any oil) and a warm washcloth instead of disposable make-up wipes. There are online tutorials showing how to make your own make-up remover pads or you can buy them premade.

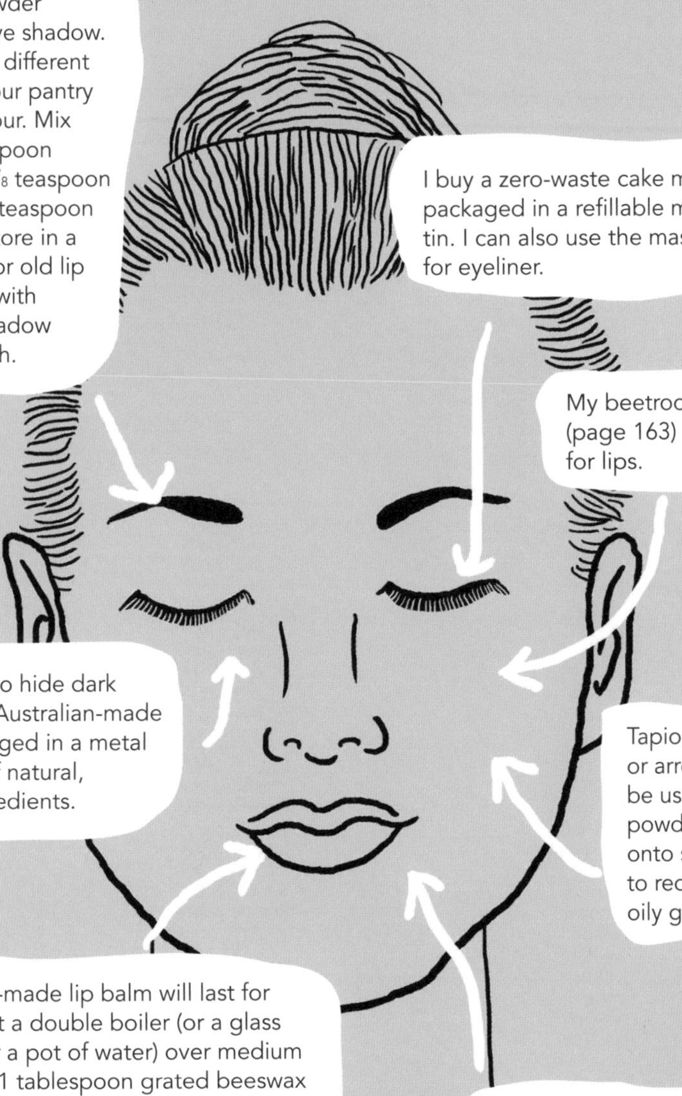

My eyebrow powder doubles as an eye shadow. Experiment with different ingredients in your pantry for the right colour. Mix together $^{1}/_{4}$ teaspoon carob powder, $^{1}/_{8}$ teaspoon turmeric and $^{1}/_{8}$ teaspoon cinnamon and store in a small container or old lip balm tin. Apply with a regular eye-shadow or eyebrow brush.

I buy a zero-waste cake mascara packaged in a refillable metal tin. I can also use the mascara for eyeliner.

My beetroot cheek stain (page 163) also works for lips.

On days I want to hide dark circles, I use an Australian-made concealer packaged in a metal tin, consisting of natural, cruelty-free ingredients.

Tapioca powder or arrowroot can be used as face powder. Brushed onto skin, it helps to reduce any oily glow.

My home-made lip balm will last for a year. Set a double boiler (or a glass bowl over a pot of water) over medium heat. Put 1 tablespoon grated beeswax and 4 tablespoons olive oil into the top of the boiler (or the glass bowl) and stir until the beeswax has melted and both have combined. Pour into a container or old lip balm tin to set.

I use a lipstick housed in a compostable cardboard tube, made of natural ingredients, which also works for cheeks.

BEETROOT CHEEK STAIN

My first DIY experiment with home-made blush did not go as smoothly as the mascara. I had read everywhere about beetroot powder being a wonderful natural colouring, but getting it unpackaged was hard. I looked into making my own: all I had to do was slice beetroot finely, dry it in an oven and then blend into a powder. I followed the directions, placed the dried beetroot into my blender, put the lid on and turned the dial – then looked on in horror as beetroot dust flew about my kitchen. As I began wiping up the powder, the water on the cloth turned the powder into a wet paste; soon I was smearing it everywhere. I later found out this can typically happen, after reading several comments about the same disaster on various instructions for making beetroot powder.

By this stage I tried not to get frustrated with the beetroot calamity, choosing to keep going to make what remained of my beetroot powder into blush. The beetroot blush was applied to the apples of my cheeks but the powder settled into my pores, making me look dirty. I then tried mixing it with arrowroot powder but found it didn't sit on my face correctly. When I used the rest of the powder as a natural lip colour, the grainy texture looked odd and didn't feel nice.

I eventually found a simpler way to make cheek colouring that actually works for me.

1 beetroot
¼ teaspoon vodka

Peel and grate the beetroot.

Use your hands to squeeze the grated beetroot over a bowl (the juice will stain clothing). Pour the liquid through a strainer, collecting only the juice.

Measure out 2 teaspoons of the beetroot juice and add to the vodka.

Using a small funnel pour into a bottle – I store mine in an old essential oil bottle with an orifice dropper. It will last for 2 months stored in the fridge.

DEODORANTS

These days I don't wear deodorant or antiperspirants, as much for the over-packaging as their unnecessarily long list of ingredients. But let's wind back and talk about armpits, sweat and smell. I had to learn about how this area worked to believe that my own deodorant recipe would be okay and not render me friendless.

Armpits are made up of sweat glands and hair. The area also generates heat, explaining why you see people fold their arms and put their hands near their armpits on colder days. The sweat glands produce sweat throughout the day. If you are exercising, then you will produce more sweat; sitting still will mean less sweat production. When The Builder and I started trying low-waste deodorant options, we found a popular bicarb (baking soda) version left us with a red rash. (This doesn't happen to everyone, as everyone's skin is different.) In between experiments, when The Builder was using no deodorant, we discovered he didn't actually smell unless he was doing rigorous manual work or after a bike ride. Some people don't smell by way of their genetics, diet or hair; and some people can be much more sensitive in their ability to detect smells, too. Before trying a low-waste deodorant, give your underarms a break for two weeks to see – or smell – if there is a difference.

There is one thing that we all have in common that creates a smell: bacteria. It's completely normal, so don't freak out. The best way to help eliminate smell is to wash really well. I wash my armpits in the morning and before I go to bed at night with soap and water. Simply by washing your armpits thoroughly, you will likely find using home-made deodorant successful.

Don't stress if the thought of making your own deodorant doesn't sound appealing. There are many ready-made low-waste deodorants available in glass or tin packaging – I have listed several in the Directory (page 258).

> **Fact**
> Sweat does not smell – it is the bacteria on our bodies that causes the smell.

> **Fact**
> When the word 'fragrance' is listed in a product's ingredients, it can mean the existence of dozens of individual ingredients.

BICARBONATE OF SODA DEODORANT

Some people may find they have a reaction to bicarb – make sure to test on a small area first.

55 g (2 oz/¼ cup)
    bicarbonate of soda
    (baking soda)
95 g (3¼ oz/¼ cup)
    arrowroot, tapioca or
    cornflour (cornstarch)
2–3 tablespoons coconut oil
10 drops tea tree oil
    (optional)

Mix the bicarbonate of soda and arrowroot (or alternatives) in a bowl. Add the coconut oil and tea tree oil (if using). Start with 1½ tablespoons of the coconut oil; add more if you want a runnier paste.

Scoop the mixture into a sterilised wide-mouth glass jar (see page 98).

To use, scoop a pea-size amount for each underarm and wipe over the area. Store in a cool, dark place for up to a year.

BICARB-FREE DEODORANT

4 tablespoons coconut oil
1 tablespoon shea butter
1½ tablespoons grated
    beeswax
3 tablespoons arrowroot,
    tapioca or cornstarch
10 drops tea tree oil

Heat a double boiler (or a glass bowl fitted above a pot of water) on the stove-top. Combine the coconut oil, beeswax and shea butter in the top of the double boiler (or bowl).

Heat until the beeswax has melted and all the ingredients are combined. Remove the top of the double boiler (or bowl) from the heat. Add the tea tree oil and the arrowroot.

Stir until all the ingredients are mixed together.

Scoop into a sterilised wide-mouth glass jar (see page 98).

To use, scoop a pea-size amount for each underarm and wipe over the area. Store in a cool, dark place for up to a year.

SIMPLE VINEGAR DEODORANT

This is the deodorant that The Builder and I use now. The vinegar it contains helps to kill bacteria. If you're worried about the smell, it disappears within an hour.

Mix 125 ml (4 fl oz/½ cup) apple-cider vinegar with 125 ml (4 fl oz/½ cup) water in a spray bottle and shake to combine.

If you have a smaller bottle, just keep the vinegar and water in the same proportions: a half-bottle of each.

PERFUME

Modern fragrance bottles are a complex packaging item. Made up of glass or crystal, plastic and aluminium, plus the cardboard box they come in, you'd probably believe you're paying for the packaging over the contents. A bottle of perfume, eau de toilet or cologne is hard to dispose of through recycling; they often end up in landfill.

Fragrance companies are not required to provide information on the contents of what makes up their fragrances. While they will describe what the fragrance will smell like (roses, gardenias, orange, musk and so on) there is no law to let the customer know if there are synthetic properties, hidden preservatives or anything that could cause an allergy or rash.

A simple swap from store-bought perfume is to try essential oils. Essential oils are the aromatic essence of the plant or flower distilled by steam or water, with no hidden ingredients. Essential oils are rarely referred to as a fragrance because they contain therapeutic benefits: for example, lavender essential oil is considered calming. There are many books available on how to mix essential oils to create your own perfume. If you'd like to have a go, here are some suggested essential oil blends:

☐ orange, jasmine and sandalwood

☐ bergamot, rose, jasmine and sandalwood

☐ lemongrass, lime, lavender and vetiver

☐ sweet marjoram, lavender and ylang-ylang

Most recycling facilities can find it hard to recycle the orifice dropper and lid of essential oil bottles, as they are sometimes too small and can be missed during the sorting process. Instead, place them inside a plastic bottle until half full, then put the whole bottle into your recycling bin. It could be worth seeking out local essential oil companies to see if they will allow for refills of your essential oil bottles. Just make sure the bottles are cleaned thoroughly before refilling them.

MENSTRUATION

We can't talk about the body without talking about menstrual products. Every year, over 45 billion feminine hygiene products are disposed of and, on average, a conventional pad contains the plastic equivalent of five plastic bags. Including packaging, that is a lot of unnecessary waste going to landfill when you consider there are safe and healthy alternatives that will also save money. I'm talking about menstrual cups and cloth pads. You'd be forgiven for not even knowing what these are. I don't remember learning about these options, but they've existed since before I was born. Over the course of five years I have saved over $500 on sanitary products alone and I never have to rush to the store if I'm ever caught out.

Menstrual cups are made of medical-grade silicone and designed for reuse. They are similar in shape to an egg cup, and hold more blood than the standard heavy-flow tampon. A menstrual cup will last up to 10 years with care and maintenance. To use, simply fold in half and insert as you would a tampon. The silicone cup collects the blood and, depending on flow, there should be no leaking. Rinse out thoroughly between uses.

The design of a cloth pad looks the same as a commercial pad but, instead of plastic tape made with adhesive chemicals to hold it in place, a cloth pad comes with metal press studs on the wings that fold and clip around your underwear. The pads usually consist of layers of cotton fleece and flannel, making them soft, comfortable and, importantly, breathable. They come in a variety of patterns and cater for heavy, normal and light flows. The pads can be washed by hand or just placed in a washing machine, not requiring any special treatment. I have a cute mermaid-print wash and carry bag for when I'm out and about.

Period underwear is another option that's becoming popular. This is where you bleed freely onto specially designed underwear to use during your time of the month. The crotch of period underwear contains layers of cotton fleece to absorb the blood. Period underwear caters more for lighter days or women with a light flow. They can work in conjunction with a menstrual cup or cloth pads. See the Directory (page 258) for some recommendations.

TOILET PAPER

Beware toilet paper packs wrapped in paper: it generally has a sneaky plastic lining. This is a hygiene rule for toilet paper sold in packs in Australia. Individually wrapped rolls means there is usually no sneaky plastic. Who Gives A Crap (WGAC; the company funds clean-water projects) and Pure Planet (PP; tree-free paper using sugarcane and bamboo pulp waste) sell toilet paper individually wrapped in paper, shipped from China. If you feel inclined to order, suggest they try using a plastic-free tape (the more people who ask, the higher the chance they will make the swap). WGAC and PP claim to contain no BPA, which gets into recycled toilet paper through store receipts placed in recycling bins. If you are keen to go paper-free, look into family cloth (reusable toilet paper) and bidets.

MEDICINE

While I have listed a small handful of simple cold remedies here, I try to steer clear of looking too far into medical packaging. If you would like to dive deeper, I suggest doing your own research. Just remember: without our health we have nothing, and plastic has enabled advancements in treatment and care.

One swap you can make is to dispose of medication properly. When medicines get into the environment via our toilets, sinks or landfills, they can pose a threat. In Australia, medicines can be returned to any community pharmacy for correct disposal; you don't have to go to the original pharmacy.

> **Tip**
> Swap bandaids for cloth bandages or choose a recycled plastic bandaid like those made by Everyday Good Co.

SORE THROAT GARGLE

When a sore throat comes along, I visit my herb garden for sage to make this gargle and will also add it to an onion and honey concoction to eat throughout the day. Sage's antiseptic and astringent properties help to soothe inflamed throats.

2 tablespoons sage leaves
(or 1 tablespoon dried)
1 tablespoon salt
60 ml (2 fl oz/¼ cup)
apple-cider vinegar

Add the sage leaves and 250 ml (8½ fl oz/1 cup) hot water (not boiling) to a cup and let steep for 20 minutes

Add the salt and apple-cider vinegar.

Let cool to a comfortable temperature to gargle. Use throughout the day until symptoms reduce.

COLD-FIGHTING TONIC

I have started seeing similar versions of this traditional remedy popping up at health food stores.

1¼ litres (42 fl oz/5 cups)
apple-cider vinegar
1 onion, chopped and peeled
3 garlic cloves
2 tablespoons turmeric
2 tablespoons ginger
4 tablespoons grated horse-radish
1/8 teaspoon cayenne
pepper (optional)
330 g (12 oz/1 cup) honey

In a large sterilized glass jar (see page 98), add the vinegar, onion, garlic, turmeric, horseradish and cayenne (if using). Seal the jar and store in a warm area of your house for 2 weeks. With a sieve, strain the liquid (compost the rest). Pour the liquid back into the jar and add the honey. Give it a good shake, then store in the fridge. At the first sign of a cold, take 1 tablespoon every 2 hours or add 2 tablespoons to a mug of warm water and sip.

EUCALYPTUS STEAM BATH

To unblock a nose or clear out sinus congestion I always turn to a eucalyptus steam bath.

Pour 1¼ litres (42 fl oz/5 cups) hot water into a bowl, then add 1 drop eucalyptus oil.

Place a towel over your head and bring your face over the bowl, creating a tent.

Inhale the steam for 10 minutes with eyes closed.

BEAUTY + BODY TOP TIPS

CHANGE ONE THING

Swap your bottle of body wash for an unpackaged
or paper-wrapped bar of soap – it will keep you clean,
cost less and last longer.

CHANGE TWO THINGS

When you next have to replace your toothbrush
or razor, choose a sustainable option. A bamboo
toothbrush can be composted, and a safety razor
will last you forever.

CHANGE THE WORLD

Look at the beauty and body items you use the most
often and have a go at making your own, using pantry
items and customising with your favourite natural
colours or scents. Team up with friends and make
a day of it!

ENTERTAINING
+ EVENTS

Choosing meaningful experiences and spending time with the people we love has become one of the peak benefits of zero-waste living for me. And whether we are celebrating birthdays, sharing festive cheer or just having a barbecue, there are many ways to keep waste to a minimum.

All events require planning; a low-waste event simply has an extra layer of planning. Many of us already own or can easily source alternatives to the throwaway items or plastic-packaged food that have sadly become mainstays of 'easy' entertaining. To start planning how to reduce rubbish at events, whether it's something we host ourselves or a function held by others, it's useful to divide the event into different categories according to the type of waste likely to be produced, for example:

 invitations and cards

 food and drink

☐ decorating

☐ gifts

With some practice and forward thinking, you'll no longer have to creep out on bin night following a party with a plastic bag full of rubbish, frantically looking up and down the street for a neighbour's bin to cram your excess waste into because yours is too full. (We've all been there, right?)

> **Fact**
>
> In the US, household waste increases by an extra 25 per cent between Thanksgiving and Christmas.

INVITATIONS + CARDS

I love receiving beautifully designed invitations and cards. Having worked as a graphic designer for more than a decade, I've also created a fair amount myself. A background in visual communications has meant that I've been privy to the many different ways to create and send a print invitation or card while keeping waste to a minimum.

But first, remember that sharing details of an event via a phone call or face to face are both simple ways to reduce waste, while also providing the chance to catch up with family and friends. The same goes when it comes to saying thanks for a gift, or recognising a birthday or festive period – why not leave the card and instead try to catch up with the person?

The internet is another great medium for sending out invitations or greetings. With more and more platforms developed each year, there is no shortage of ways to set up an event. For barbecues, dinners and even my wedding rehearsal, I've used Facebook. Events can be created privately, with themes, links and space to ask questions and share information. There are many online invitation platforms allowing custom design, or users can choose from a range of thoughtfully designed stationery templates with matching 'envelopes' and the ability to manage a guest list and gift registries. We found online invitation platforms a great way to manage a big event like our wedding, and many friends have used various e-invite platforms for their own weddings, engagements, baby showers, birthday parties and anniversary celebrations. You could also have a traditional invitation, containing all necessary details, designed and sent as a PDF attached to an email.

Not everyone has access to the internet, or you might prefer to send paper invites or cards via post. Most designers and printers will be able to help you find 100 per cent sustainable recycled post-consumer paper for your invitations, cards and envelopes. If you are designing and printing your own at home, all specialty paper stores will either have recycled papers in stock or can source them for you. Otherwise look for ready-made options that are free of glitter, ribbons or other embellishments, preferably printed with soy or vegetable inks on recycled paper.

Tip

Choose old-fashioned lick-and-stick postage stamps, as they come without the extra shiny paper surrounds that stickers have.

FOOD + DRINK

Food and drink at events often seems to involve a lot of rubbish – think dishes covered in plastic wrap, individually portioned desserts in plastic cups, packets of chips and cans of drink. And there's often so much food left over!

To make the planning process easy when it comes to catering for an event without the waste, I take two pieces of scrap paper, both divided into two columns. On one piece of paper, the first column contains the dishes I plan to serve and the second column helps me plan out what serving dishes I need. If I need any extra crockery or catering equipment, these will be added to my shopping list with an action to purchase, borrow or hire.

On the other piece of paper, I write the ingredients I need to purchase broken up by store in the first column. In the second column, I list the appropriate containers, bags and jars I'll need to collect the food. Make sure you're putting extra thought into how many people will be eating and how much food you'll actually need.

Tip

Choosing shared dishes made of local, seasonal food helps keep food waste to a minimum, as guests can choose how much they want to eat.

A: dishes	B: serving dishes
lemonade	3 x pitchers from home
dips and crackers	bowls and breadboard from home
mini quiches	platter (borrow or buy second-hand)

A: bulk store ingredients	B: containers/bags/jars
olive oil	glass bottle
cumin	small spice jar

A: market ingredients	B: containers/bags/jars
lemons	cloth bag
mint leaves	cloth bag

THREE-INGREDIENT CRACKERS

Chips and crackers can be hard to find unpackaged, even at a bulk store. Here is my simple three-ingredient cracker recipe (I'm including the water). Add herbs and spices to create different flavours.

150 g (5½ oz/1 cup) plain (all-purpose) flour (any plain flour you want)
3 tablespoons olive oil

Preheat oven to 200°C (400°F).

Combine the flour and olive oil in a bowl. The mixture will be crumbly.

Add tablespoons of cold water, one at a time, up to 4 tablespoons, until you get a dough-like consistency. Depending on the flour, you might not need all 4 tablespoons of water or you may need more.

Break the dough up into four equal parts and roll out until thin (around 2 mm/⅛ in). I use a pasta machine but a rolling pin or a even wine bottle will do the job.

Cut the crackers into desired shapes. Lay them on a lightly greased baking tray and bake in the oven for 6–8 minutes, until golden and crispy.

LEMONADE

We made this refreshing homemade lemonade to serve at our wedding, with the help of family and friends. It is one of my favourite memories from the wedding preparations – mainly because of The Builder's panicking, thinking we would never have enough. In the end, we made more than enough and were able to freeze the excess concentrate to enjoy the following summer. To up the reusing element with this recipe, zest the lemon rind before juicing the lemons and freeze the zest in ice-cube trays for later use in dishes like couscous or cakes.

250 ml (8½ fl oz/1 cup) freshly squeezed lemon juice
230 g (8 oz/1 cup) caster (superfine) sugar
2 teaspoons orange-blossom water or rosewater (optional)
mint leaves, to serve

Combine lemon juice and sugar in a jug, stirring until sugar has dissolved, to create a concentrate.

Add the orange-blossom water or rosewater, if using.

If serving immediately, add 1½ litres (51 fl oz/6 cups) water and scatter the mint leaves over. Otherwise pour the concentrate into a jar and freeze for later use.

Instead of resorting to bottles and cans, fun low-waste party drinks can be made in advance. Simple cordials and lemonade require an hour of preparation while others, like a ginger beer or a sparkling fruit wine, will need more time. Even water can be dressed up, using herbs from the garden, or perhaps some leftover food scraps from meal prep. Try infusing water with the tops of strawberries, slices of cucumber, oranges rinds, mint or sprigs of thyme.

There is a growing trend from wineries, craft breweries and specialty bottle shops to offer tapped beer and wine refills; it's best to call ahead to see what is available and if they have designated times. In some instances, customers need to buy the first bottle by law, which can be refilled endlessly. Another option is to hire a keg of beer or wine for a big event. Check the internet for any places that offer this in your neighbourhood, or ask at your local bottle shop.

We all have those friends who'll want to bring along a plate or bottle of something. Rather than enforce a hard rule against guests' generosity so you can avoid bringing rubbish into your home, set up bins to minimise what could end up in landfill. Gather used boxes to help sort the soft plastic, hard plastic, other plastic, glass, aluminium, paper and compost. Placing the 'rubbish' bin out of the way will encourage guests to save materials from landfill while prompting conversation too. And ask guests to bring along an empty container or lend out your own so they can take any extra food home.

For some big events, you could be lucky enough to have a professional caterer. Try looking for a caterer who is willing to work with you on creating less waste – just ask! You might have to guide them through the process, but this can be done by simply writing a list of what you'd like to achieve and ways they can assist in their operations.

Tip

In the weeks leading up to big events like Christmas, defrost and eat the contents of your freezer so it will be empty and ready to store those yummy leftovers.

Fact

In some states of Australia, bottles and cans can be returned to a depot for a small refund; in these states, drink containers makes up less than 3 per cent of landfill, compared to up to 13 per cent elsewhere. Trading your containers for cash surely eases the woes of cleaning up after a party!

TABLEWARE

I can admit to buying and then forgetting about plastic plates, bowls, cups and cutlery, with half-used or even full packets stuffed away in cupboards while I went on to buy more for the next event. The popular single-use plastic tableware sold at supermarkets is made either of non-foamed polystyrene, polyethylene or other plastics. If they're not forgotten in cupboards, these items sit in landfill, unable to biodegrade, or worse, are placed into or beside overflowing bins in public areas where they risk escaping into the environment.

Thankfully, throwaway plastic can be easily swapped for the real reusable deal. For example, we spent an afternoon collecting small plates and glassware from several second-hand stores for a Christmas barbecue, avoiding single-use plastic plates and cups without breaking the bank. Rather than donating the items back to charity, we held onto them for future get-togethers. Another option is to encourage guests to bring their own tableware. Try making it a fun challenge by setting a 'crazy glass' theme, directing guests to visit their local second-hand store to pick up something outlandish.

Another reason to swap out the disposable plastics is to avoid the risk of serving up phthalates and other ingredients from the plastic with our food. When plastic is heated by way of a microwave, dishwasher or holding hot food, the high temperatures help many of the chemicals break free and they are fond of latching themselves onto fatty foods. The possible threat of plastics to my health was enough for me to ditch the flimsy plastic plates, bowls and cutlery too. If the thought of taking ceramic crockery to a park for a barbecue is unappealing, second-hand stores will generally stock melamine picnicware, but just use it for cold foods.

What about paper or bamboo plates?
Compared to plastic, paper and bamboo plates are the kinder choice for the environment, especially those made of post-consumer waste (recycled) rather than virgin wood-based fibres (new trees). You can make them an even better choice by disposing of them properly, ideally in a compost, as they will produce more methane gas in landfill and the residual food and grease makes them difficult to recycle. Unfortunately there are rarely compost bins available at parties or public events to make responsible disposal easy.

What about bioplastics or biodegradable plates?

Plates, bowls and cutlery made of bioplastics and biodegradable plastics are designed to break down eventually with the help of UV rays, warm temperatures, the environment and micro-organisms. The terms *bioplastic* and *biodegradable* are very different, and I'll happily admit they can be confusing. I wouldn't blame anyone if they saw the letters 'bio' at the start of a word and assumed this meant the material could break down as quickly as something like an apple core, but that's not quite the case.

Bioplastics are made from corn, sugar and other plant material. Neither an apple core nor a bioplastic plate will break down in landfill properly without producing methane gas. Since not all bioplastics are made the same, some might break down in a backyard compost while others require high temperatures, similar to those found in an industrial compost. Unfortunately, this information is never available on the packaging, and services have not been set up to capture the resources from landfill. When a bioplastic ends up in the environment, it's more likely to break up quickly into smaller pieces. These smaller pieces can pose a greater risk to wildlife and still take years to break down – and, even then, they can leave hazardous residues.

Biodegradable plastics have the same material base as regular plastic, just with additives to help them break down when exposed to oxygen and sunlight. Buried deep within a landfill site, they are deprived of both. The other catch is that many of these plastics are tested for biodegradability within industrial composting facilities and not the natural environment. Countries like Australia, the UK and the US have standards that define what can be called biodegradable, but there is still not consistent testing.

The companies making these products – and the people buying them – are trying to do the right thing by having products that don't hang around for thousands of years. Unfortunately, the fact that they're disposable is still symptomatic of our one-time-use, throwaway mentality. Part of the challenge of reducing your waste is to break that mentality. If in doubt, choose reusables instead.

Fact

Most plastic cutlery is made from polystyrene, the same plastic used to make expanded polystyrene foam. It's hard to recycle, and usually ends up in landfill, where it won't break down.

Tip

Plastic straws and cocktail mixers can be swapped for reusable metal versions or gone without – keep this in mind when you're at a restaurant or bar too!

DECORATING

Dressing up our homes or venues for a party is a way to get creative while setting a fun mood or theme for an event. Instead of reaching for the stock-standard balloons or plastic novelties, there are many other ways to decorate without everything ending up in the bin afterwards. The possibilities of using items from nature and up-cycling old materials into something new are endless when decorating for an event. I've learned how to make Christmas crackers from old toilet paper rolls, recycled-paper party hats for birthdays and reusable cloth advent calendars full of activities or unwrapped treats bought from bulk stores.

Choosing natural decorations of flowers and foliage is a low-waste option we often use when entertaining. Vegetables, fruits and plants can be woven into wreaths, set up as table decorations and placed on cakes. Dried fruits like citrus and cranberries, as well as pieces of cooked popcorn, look very sweet threaded together and strung up as garlands. Last year my sister made salt dough Christmas ornaments with her son using old ribbon to hang them.

If you enjoy getting crafty, most cities have craft rescue or salvage stores where craft supplies have been saved from landfill and sold at a discounted price. To find one close to you, search the internet or call local craft stores.

Not all of us love to spend our time crafting decorations; instead, support the local community by having a rummage through second-hand stores, local markets or men's sheds for old or hand-made decorations and even gifts.

> **Tip**
>
> Marquees, trestle tables and extra chairs are now available so cheaply at some stores that they could almost be considered disposable. Instead, ask to borrow from family and friends or hire what you need.

> **Tip**
>
> Swap the traditional Christmas tree for a native plant. Transfer it to the garden in the new year or keep in a pot until next Christmas. If you do use a pine tree, don't forget to compost it or cut it up for the green waste bin. Remember, if you already own something like a plastic Christmas tree and decorations, keep using them. Making use of what we already own is the least wasteful and most sustainable choice.

GIFTS

There are many celebrations throughout the year with a big emphasis on gift giving. More than half of all Australians have admitted to throwing away one Christmas gift a year, and I'll admit that in the past I certainly got rid of gifts that I deemed useless. One item in particular was a strawberry slicer I was gifted by a work colleague after I tried to tell them I didn't want a gift. It squashed my strawberries and was ridiculous to clean! Off it went to landfill.

Receiving and giving presents can be lovely, especially when they are gifted with intention and kind thought. Rather than put an absolute ban on gifts, I now offer family, friends and co-workers a list of options. This also creates another opportunity to discuss and share the zero-waste and plastic-free lifestyle.

Unnecessary gifts made of cheap disposable materials with little use can be avoided by asking some questions. If you want to give something to someone ask these questions (or flip them on yourself when asking for a gift – or when making any other type of purchase):

☐ Do they really need this?

☐ Is it useful?

☐ Where was it made and what materials were used?

☐ Was it ethically made under fair working conditions?

☐ Could I buy it second-hand?

☐ What will happen at the end of its life: can it be recycled or reused, or is it destined for landfill?

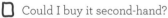

During festive periods, setting up a gift swap with your family, friends and co-workers makes giving gifts fun – and you'll only have to organise one present. Secret Santa involves everyone putting their names into a hat. Each person pulls out a name. This person receiving the gift has no idea who will be buying, making or organising a gift for them. On the day of gift giving, all gifts are snuck into a location and eventually passed to the recipient by someone in the group.

Bad Santa is similar to Secret Santa, but instead of pulling names out of a hat, everyone brings a random gift and sneaks it into the gift area. During the gift exchange, participants receive a number each. Number one is the first to step forward and choose a gift, then unwrap it for everyone to see. Next, the person who pulled out number two steps forward; if this person likes what number one has, number one is forced to swap it with them and open a new gift, otherwise number two opens a new gift. And so it continues until all gifts have been opened and swapped. In my family we love Bad Santa: the fun of not knowing what gift you'll end up with makes the exchange more enjoyable. Put a rule in place that gifts must be second-hand or hand-made.

Here are some of my favourite low-waste gift ideas (there are also some ideas for kids on page 212).

- movie, theatre, sporting or concert tickets
- dinner voucher
- yoga pass
- weekend away
- visit to an art gallery or museum
- driving range or mini golf
- cooking class
- home-made food like jams, relish, chutneys, sauces or biscuits
- home-made bath soak or body scrub
- plants and seeds
- artwork
- donation to a charity on their behalf

Tip

When you are choosing a gift, try choosing experiences over things, and don't be afraid of 'regifting'.

GIFTWRAPPING

The least wasteful way to present a gift would be to simply hide it, unwrapped, behind your back before giving, but some of us enjoy watching our recipients thrill in the unwrapping of a gift. I have memories from Christmases gone by, after the presents had been unwrapped, of giant plastic balls of tape torn from the paper in our excited state to get our toys out. Now imagine all the plastic tape balls across the world, more than likely sitting in landfill.

Plastic tape is made of, well, plastic, with one side covered in an adhesive solvent to allow for the sticking and holding together of materials. Most recycling facilities will take paper and cardboard with tape on them, but this does not mean the tape is recycled. As the cardboard and paper are turned back into pulp with the addition of liquid, the plastic tape rises to the top of the mixture; it is scooped off, then sent to landfill.

I have seen plastic tape made of recycled plastic in a stationery store, but this plastic, like most, is down-cycled, meaning it can't be recycled again. There is another tape that looks exactly the same as plastic tape but is called cellulose tape. Cellulose is made from the fibres of plant matter with petroleum-free or solvent-free adhesive to create the stickiness. The cellulose is more likely to break down with the paper during the recycling process compared to plastic tape.

Depending on brands, gummed paper and masking tape are the least wasteful of all the tapes since paper can be recycled up to ten times, although I have yet to come across 100 per cent recycled gummed paper or masking tape. Look for solvent-free masking tape with natural rubber adhesive. Gummed paper can be bought from large and small stationery stores and online. Visit the Directory (page 261) for websites selling low-waste stationery alternatives.

My preference is for twine or wool, discarded ribbons and cloth scraps in lieu of tape. Unlike tape, they can be used again and again, up-cycled or composted (depending if the material is natural or a manufactured synthetic).

Glue is another option, but instead of using store-bought plastic-packaged glue, it's very easy to make your own. Just mix together a tablespoon of water for every tablespoon of plain (all-purpose) flour and you're ready to start sticking!

Old magazines, newspaper and atlas pages, or even children's artwork, all make great wrapping – be sure to check the ink does not rub off from the newspaper, to avoid the gift being stained.

Foraged leaves make cute gift tags or even table settings (we used these at our wedding).

Reusable cloth bags made from excess fabric or the Japanese furoshiki (page 188) are a simple way to promote reusable wrapping for many years to come.

Remove the front of old Christmas or birthday cards and reuse as decorations or tags by simply folding or cutting in half.

The lure of brown paper packages tied up with compostable twine is a simple compromise for those wanting to stay traditional.

POTATO STAMPS + BEETROOT INK

Make sure to let the receiver know that your stamped paper can be reused, composted or recycled with a little note.

Cut a potato in half. Wipe away any moisture on the cut side that you'll be using for the stamp.

With a pencil, draw a love heart, circle, star, Christmas tree or letter from the alphabet on the cut side of the potato.

Take a knife and begin cutting away the flesh of the potato around the image you have drawn. You want the stamp to have a raised area of 5–10 mm (¼–½ in). Put the potato to the side once you are happy with the stamp you have cut out.

Next, take a beetroot and begin grating over a large bowl. Once the beetroot is fully grated, remove the grater and squeeze the beetroot with your hands. If you are not afraid to have stained hands for a couple of hours, you can do this without gloves, otherwise use rubber gloves.

Scoop out the grated beetroot to the side. Save it to cook with or compost. There should be a lovely rich red juice left in the bottom of the bowl.

Dip the cut side of the potato – your stamp – into the beetroot ink or use a paintbrush to brush the ink onto your stamp. Now, start stamping.

FUROSHIKI

Furoshiki is the art of wrapping and carrying items with a piece of cloth. I love furoshiki for its versatility: wrapping books, food or even wine bottles in beautiful fabric that can also work for a makeshift picnic or just to dry your hands. While there is traditional furoshiki cloth available, tea towels (dish towels), second-hand scarves or material off-cuts will work.

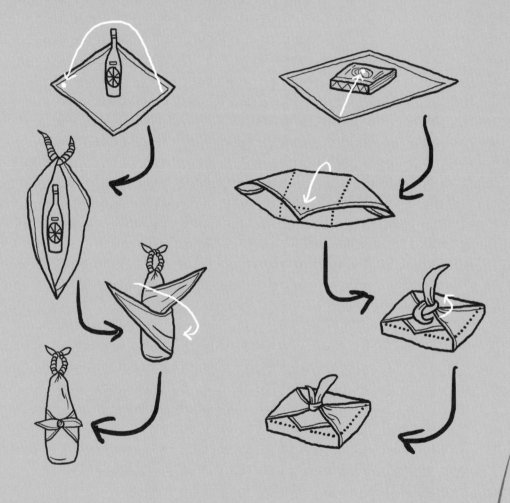

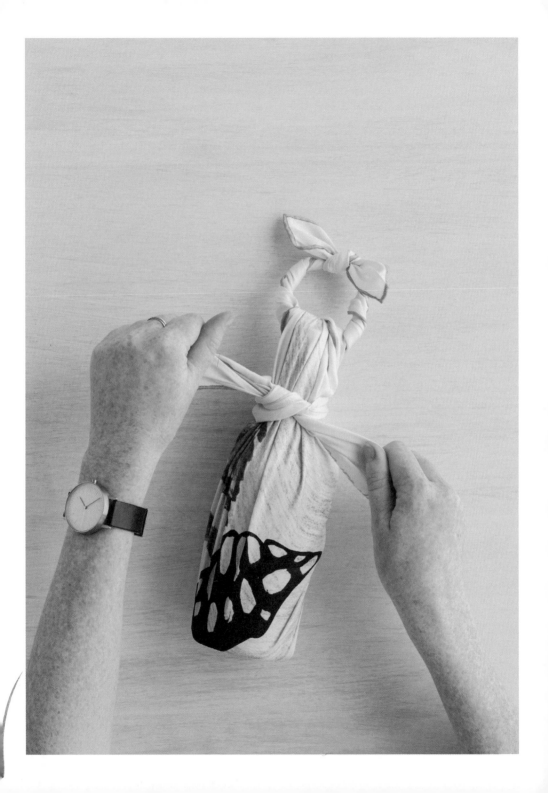

LAURA ISSELL

Designer, stylist and event manager at Put Your Heart Into It

In 2013 I was returning from Malaysia by boat, and mooring outside what appeared to be a pristine island. Upon the beach, a scattering of people stood along the shoreline; as the distance reduced, the beachcombers revealed themselves to be not people at all, but sculptures; hulking figures amassed from the surrounding debris: thousands of uncoupled thongs and carcinogenic rainbows of cigarette lighters.

I spent hours on that beach collecting rubbish and, having nowhere to dispose of it myself, created my own sculpture, an absurd beauty, incongruous to this landscape that deserved only purity. It was my first realisation of how deeply we have forgotten where our waste can end up.

These days, through my job as an event stylist, I'm able to create events while helping raise awareness of sustainable food sourcing and waste reduction, creating important dialogue and eliciting change, while treading gently on the earth. Here are some simple tricks you could consider for your next event so you can do your bit by setting an example of how parties should be done!

TIPS FOR ZERO-WASTE EVENTS

☐ Let your guests know you are coordinating a sustainable event: suggest carpooling or public transport and give them a chance to contribute.

☐ If you keep only minimal plates, glasses and cutlery in your home, call ahead and ask someone to bring an extra set rather than buying more. (Washing up really doesn't take that long if allocated to a handful of people – it can even be fun!)

☐ Why not make dips from scratch? There's more to go around, they taste a darn sight better, you will use less packaging and hello leftovers!

☐ Search second-hand stores and online community groups for what you need instead of buying new. There is always an abundance of things that have nothing wrong with them. It's surprisingly easy to buy second-hand candles, cushions, chairs and vases online when someone is finished with them from a previous event.

☐ Have a tablecloth or large piece of fabric you love but don't use? How about turning it into handmade fabric napkins, or dropping it off to a local dressmaker and asking them to cut and sew them? You'll reduce the amount of paper napkins used, and you'll create something that is uniquely you.

☐ When purchasing decorations, ask yourself if you will use them more than a handful of times and where they will end up when the event is over. Inspect the quality and consider if you really need them. Think about decorating with something you can leave up permanently, such as solar lights, or utilising things you already have at home, like newspaper or old wrapping paper to make signs or bunting.

☐ When buying flowers, please stop and ask your florist if their flowers are imported; if so, don't purchase them. Local flowers haven't travelled so far to get to you and will last longer than a week – especially natives. Request no wrapping please! A piece of string will do the trick and you can use it again. If all else fails – living plants in pots are the answer. Who doesn't love lush green foliage? And you can pop the plants back in your home or give them as a gift after the event.

WHAT TO DO WHEN YOU'RE THE GUEST

The scenario: you've been invited to a barbecue at the house of a friend who is in no way on the road to low-waste living. You know there is a chance the food will come packaged, there will possibly be single-use cutlery, plates and cups and no compost. Rather than become disgruntled or refuse all invitations, turn the thought around and look at the situation differently: your family and friends would like to have you over, enjoy time together and share some food with you. They are not having a party to make rubbish; it's just that the hosts might not be aware of the simple swaps to reduce waste.

Six months into my low-waste journey, I found myself at a party where I was enjoying a lovely home-made dip with a thinly sliced French bread stick. As I commented on the dip and how clever it was to use a bread stick instead of buying packaged crackers, my host went on to confess the dip had actually been bought in plastic and transferred to a bowl, as had been most of the other food she had out. She started apologising profusely for all the plastic, as she knew I was trying to reduce my usage. I felt horrible for making her feel bad. From that day forward, I decided to leave other people to make their own choices rather than potentially make some feel guilty. I've found family and friends have made changes just by seeing how I live my life, adopting what works for them.

As a guest, you could choose to call ahead to let the host know you're trying to reduce your waste, but also let them know they don't need to go out of their way. You could bring your own cutlery, plate and cup for reuse and a container to take any leftovers home if offered, and avoid obviously packaged food and drink. The Builder and I will sometimes ask if we can use a ceramic plate and glass from the host's cupboard, promising to wash and put it back before we leave. If you like to take gifts of food, try taking something unpackaged and explain where you got it from and how it was bought: for example, pick up dessert in your own containers from a bakery or sausages at the deli. Your hosts might be inspired by your choices or they might not. Either way, your goal is to not make them feel like they are bad human beings out to destroy the environment, but to show them how another way is possible.

MY LOW-WASTE WEDDING

My idea of a wedding, at least a low-waste one, involved a trip to the city registry office and a quiet lunch. While I *love* celebrating other people's weddings, planning my own never appealed to me. Out of the two of us, I'm definitely less traditional than The Builder. He wanted to have a church wedding, to watch me walk down the aisle wearing a white dress, to pose for the cheesy photos, and to end at a party-style reception. Seeing The Builder's enthusiasm for a big celebration was sweet, and we went with his dream wedding. I'm so glad we did, as the day was so much fun! As clichéd as it sounds, my wedding was one of the happiest days of my life.

We didn't advertise our wedding as an eco event, not because we didn't want to be held up all night explaining to everyone why we chose to organise a low-waste wedding but because the goal for us was to simply lead by example and prove that many of the decisions we made can be integrated into any style of wedding, even a big Lebanese–Australian wedding in the suburbs of Melbourne. Eco-weddings are often portrayed as being small, in rural locations with hand-made everything. We wanted to debunk this idea.

As with the planning for any event, we broke everything into categories – and included some new ones such as attire and entertainment – to evaluate where waste would be created. Doing this really helped us stay focused in the five months we had to prepare for the big day. We set out questions to be applied as we worked out the logistics to reduce waste in each category.

- ☐ Can we hire it?
- ☐ Can we make it?
- ☐ Can we borrow it?
- ☐ Will anyone miss it?
- ☐ Will we be sorry we didn't have it at our wedding in 5, 10 or 15 years' time?

- ☐ How was it made?
- ☐ What will happen at the end of its life?
- ☐ Can it be reused?
- ☐ Can it be composted?
- ☐ Can it be recycled?

Most of our wedding invitations were sent using an online registry website; paper invitations for those without email were printed on recycled paper, as were the wedding day programs, menus and wedding favour cards. In lieu of a physical wedding favour (a gift for guests), we chose to donate money to a charity on our guests' behalf and requested no gifts. If guests wished to give us something, we suggested a contribution to our honeymoon. This is a common practice and, while we did receive some gifts, they were all useful items given with much thought and care.

My wedding dress and shoes were bought second-hand and the jewellery was borrowed from my mother. I sold the wedding dress to another bride using one of the many online wedding dress websites and donated my shoes back to the charity store I bought them from. My wedding band was second-hand while The Builder's ring was made from old gold jewellery belonging to his grandmother from Lebanon, a lovely reminder of his heritage. There are many online stores, antique and vintage stores, pawn shops and jewellers that sell second-hand rings or those made from recycled precious metals.

At our first meeting with our catering company, we told them of our plans to reduce our rubbish; we knew that the food would probably be the biggest waste producer on the day. They loved our ethos and worked with us to make it happen. At the end of the night, they collected all leftover food in plastic buckets for us to take and compost at home along with the natural decorations we provided. We did have the option to organise a compost collection service but we didn't need it: our compost handled it well.

We hired furniture, linen and cloth napkins along with plates, bowls, cutlery and glasses and said no to plastic straws. Drinks consisted of water, home-made lemonade, kegs of beer and wine on tap; we even had bubbles on tap. This meant there were no beer or wine bottles to recycle; in fact, the only item we recycled for the whole night were the plastic bags from ice, and soft plastic that some of our hired linen came wrapped in. If we did it again, I'd remember to ask the hire company for the linen to come without the plastic.

The bridal bouquet, bridesmaids' bouquets and table decorations were a mix of foraged and seasonal flowers, set in glass jars from home and donated by friends. We used candles donated from another wedding; for table numbers, we painted directly onto some of the candle jars. The candles have since been passed onto another bride, the jars are back in my pantry full of food and preserves, the flowers composted and table settings composted or recycled.

The day was big success. We achieved a low-waste wedding without anyone being the wiser to our eco nuptials. While our aim to create an event that reflected our values was important, the main intention was for it to be as fun and memorable for us as it was for everyone else there on the day.

ENTERTAINING + EVENTS TOP TIPS

CHANGE ONE THING

Try wrapping presents using an old scarf, fabric scrap or a proper furoshiki cloth. The cloth can be reused not only for wrapping other presents but also for wrapping food for a picnic.

CHANGE TWO THINGS

Instead of disposable plates, bowls, cutlery and cups, opt for regular crockery and utensils at your next barbecue.

CHANGE THE WORLD

Gift experiences and meaningful presents rather than items people won't use or that will end up being wasted. And, when you receive a meaningful gift in return, don't send a card – pick up the phone or organise a catch-up to show them how much you've appreciated the thought they have put in!

LITTLE PEOPLE + FURRY FRIENDS

Reducing waste with little people and furry friends might seem like a contradiction. Many people think of children and animals when they think of waste, but I wonder if that's because we equate mess with rubbish – the two are very different. Having kids and pets around invites fun and with that can come mess, but that doesn't have to mean waste.

In the lead-up to the arrival of our son last year, lots of people asked how I would be able to continue a low-waste lifestyle as a parent; others just flat-out told me that I'd have no chance. At first I would ignore their words, but over time, The Builder and I began to spend many nights worrying how we would ever raise a child and keep rubbish to a minimum. Just getting prepared for the baby's arrival felt like a monumental task, and then we started thinking of its future. Would living zero waste make our child a target? Would they end up with no friends at school? What would other parents think of us?

We realised after some time that our fears were only that. The best advice we had was what I usually tell everyone about zero-waste living anyway: to lead by example and not push anything on anyone else. Yes, we have chosen to raise our son with low-waste principles and will endeavour to explain to him along the way why we might live a little differently to others, but we will do so with open ears and hearts, respecting any choices he will eventually make on his own. We can only take it one day at a time and, of course, do the best we can, with what we've got, where we are.

We don't actually have a pet in our household, but I know that animals are often treated as members of the family. And, like any family member, they can produce rubbish from food, beds, collars, toys, powders, sprays and shampoo, to name just a few, so I've also included some tips in this chapter on low-waste pet care.

PREPARING FOR A BABY

Baby stuff is not bought for long-term use. Babies grow so quickly that they can be in and out of clothes in a matter of weeks, and their fast development means that they always have different needs. Borrowing, sharing and choosing second-hand are three easy steps of the zero-waste lifestyle, and I think I would have made the choice to 'shop' for our baby this way even if we didn't live this lifestyle – it makes financial sense. Thousands of parents seem to agree, and that's why second-hand baby items are easy to find! The moment I alerted the world to my pregnancy, there was an influx of communication from parents happy to pass on, lend or sell their used baby goods without me even having to ask. The world truly does not need any more new baby things.

Of course, there are many more benefits and reasons to borrow, share and choose second-hand, beyond saving money:

- keeping items out of landfill
- avoiding new plastic
- investing in a circular system
- recognising the effort that went into making the item
- valuing the resources needed to make each item

Our bassinet was the same one I slept in when I was a baby and suited our son well until we moved him to a larger cot, which was found via Facebook buy/swap/sell. It had some teeth marks, which my son has added too. We also furnished the baby room with lamps and a comfy breastfeeding chair from the local charity store, and our change table was passed on to us from a lovely blog reader. I took my sister-in-law's pram off her hands and tracked down the matching bassinet on Ebay. My baby carrier is from Gumtree. Sheets, wraps, muslins, clothes, shoes, socks, bibs and blankets were all donated by family and friends, or supplemented by second-hand store finds. I chose not to style his room, since most of the items would be passed on eventually, but if you'd love to create a special theme, this can easily be achieved buying second-hand.

I have found Facebook buy/swap/sell groups to be the most efficient place to gather baby goods. There are niche groups for most items, and sellers are likely to provide more information and be easier

Tip

Like baby clothes, second-hand maternity wear is easy to gather from family and friends, online or from second-hand stores. Maternity wear might not appeal to you, but remember it's not forever.

to communicate with, offering more room to negotiate a fair price. Also look out for second-hand baby markets or swap parties in your area. Don't be afraid to ask lots of questions about second-hand items before committing, including if you're getting the item from family or friends. If you can, view items first, especially in the case of prams or furniture such as highchairs or change tables, to make sure they are sturdy and don't have missing or broken parts.

When it comes to rehoming baby things, you could consider donating them to charity organisations that take items for families suffering hardship; contact your local council, maternal health nurse or child health services to find a suitable option.

BABY SHOWER GIFTS

If you're hosting a baby shower, mother blessing, push party or Baby-Q, there is a high chance someone will bring along a present. As I've mentioned, rather than say no gifts to avoid the waste and plastic, I generally find it easier to offer family and friends options. You might even be the person doing the giving! See it as another way to share the zero-waste lifestyle. My gift ideas focus on the wellbeing of a new parent. It might feel more traditional to lavish the baby with gifts, but honestly, their needs are primarily the parents' needs. If the parents are doing well physically and mentally, the baby will be well looked after.

Food
Think simple dishes full of roasted root vegetables, slow-cooked meals, soups, rice, fruit and desserts. I'd advise against anything that could cause colic (gas) if mum is breastfeeding; for inspiration, look up anti-colic diets. Food can be divided up in glass jars as individual meals, ready for the freezer.

Nappy-cleaning service
There are a number of organisations that offer a service where dirty nappies are picked up, washed, dried and dropped back to tired parents. This is the kind of gift that could woo parents into trying cloth nappies too. If this is a gift that you think would be a hit (I can guarantee it would!), do double-check what detergent the nappies are washed in. Us eco mamas and papas don't want anything too harsh that will end up close to our babies' bottoms.

Tip
Ask for the serial number or product name to check safety standards and recalls before buying or borrowing items such as furniture, prams and car seats.

Tip
While our son didn't take to a soother or dummy (he seemed to prefer his fingers), we did buy one just in case, made from sustainable natural rubber that will eventually break down in the compost. You can also buy wooden soothers finished with organic beeswax or natural oils.

Massage

I have yet to meet a mum who does not have a crick in their neck and ache in their body, either left over from pregnancy or from bending over and picking up baby all day – while babies start off small, they grow quickly and pretty soon you're carrying around eight kilograms!

Your time

Offering services like cleaning dishes, vacuuming, or just visiting to watch baby while either mum or dad can have a shower, meal or nap is a thoughtful gift. The parents will also appreciate the chance to have an adult conversation – trust me!

BREASTFEEDING – OR NOT

When it comes to baby feeding, breastfeeding is obviously pretty free from packaging, but you are not less environmentally friendly if you can't breastfeed or choose not to. Breastfeeding can be hard or unavailable to some of us, or it's a path we've decided not to pursue, and that's okay. As long as both baby and mum are happy, healthy and thriving, that's all that matters.

If you are going to be breastfeeding, use the time at second-hand stores looking for baby items to buy breastfeeding-appropriate tops and dresses for the season your baby will be born into: think simple button-up shirts, wrap dresses and loose tops. My mother was smart enough to encourage me to also buy extra pyjamas so I always have some fresh ones when needed. And you will need them in the first month! Also look into reusable breast pads – they are amazing. When they land in the wash, you won't be picking the tissue off everything, like you will be with the disposable kind. Plus you'll save money and never worry about running out.

I discovered quickly that a second-hand maternity bra is the one thing that is hard to come by, purely because they are worn so much. If you do buy a bra during the later stages of pregnancy, look for a nursing bra with ample room for you to grow, as your breasts will fluctuate in size when the baby arrives and the milk comes. While second-hand stores might not sell nursing bras, ask friends or family if they have any that were rarely used, perhaps by someone who didn't end up breastfeeding.

> **Tip**
> Use your reusable menstrual pads post birth instead of disposable liners. For added absorbency, use your baby's nappy inserts – this was a handy suggestion that worked well for me.

BOTTLES, CUPS + PLATES

In 2013, the US followed parts of Europe to put a ban on BPA in baby bottles and sippy cups. While this move was heralded by many as a step forward, the effects of the replacement chemicals have not yet been determined. For our son's bottle, we used an old mason jar converted into a baby bottle with a silicone nipple attachment. We had a couple of mason jars already, the glass is recyclable, and I can keep using the mason jars after we are finished breastfeeding. I also love the ease of storing my expressed milk directly into the mason jar in our freezer. Glass provides better protection against contamination and is easy to disinfect by simply boiling or baking in the oven (see page 98). Milk can only be stored in the freezer for a month to meet the needs of the baby's age; when I freeze milk, I write the date on a scrap of paper and secure it to the jar with an elastic band. I put the frozen milk jars into the fridge to defrost slowly and safely before heating on the stovetop.

When it comes to giving babies their own water bottles, I recommend stainless-steel bottles with replaceable silicone lids. These reduce the exposure to BPA and serve multiple purposes over time: for instance, the bottle I'm looking to buy for our son can also be used as a snack container later on. At the moment, we also let him use a regular cup, carried in a small cotton bag when we're out and about, or we give him sips from our own bottles and glasses of water.

If you can already hear the sound of a ceramic bowl or plate breaking as a result of your baby flipping it off the table, there are other alternatives, including wood, bamboo, stainless steel and plastic. I know it might sound counterintuitive to use plastic, but second-hand stores have a heavy rotation of plastic plates and bowls, or you might already have some in a picnic set – just remember to not use with hot food to reduce leaching from the plastic. When we are outside the house, I carry our son's food in a stainless-steel container, so it doubles as a serving dish and will be used for many years to come when he's at school.

Fact

Some baby bottles are made of tempered glass, which is harder to recycle – double check with your closest recycling facility before purchasing. Otherwise, bottles can be passed on when no longer needed.

Tip

There is no need for fancy teething chew toys: a simple washcloth soaked in a cup of cold chamomile tea is the easiest low-waste option for baby to relieve some of the pain. Chamomile is known to help soothe and relax.

BABY-LED WEANING

Feeding babies and toddlers is an interesting and fun time, albeit a bit messy, especially if you choose baby-led weaning. Baby-led weaning is the complete opposite to the baby food trends of highly packaged ready-made mush in squeezable pouches or single-use containers. The idea of baby-led weaning is to just let your child feed themself as they are ready, usually the same food the parents are eating themselves, such as roasted or steamed vegetables, pasta or stir-fry. There's no purées, no extra food to be made, and no time spent sitting there, slowly spooning food into baby's mouth. Anything not eaten by our son (or smeared into his hair) can be consumed by us or put into the compost. This saves waste, time and money.

What I really love about baby-led weaning is that our son can watch us eat while we eat, and babies love to mimic. The baby also learns the true taste and texture of food. Our son loves to munch on broccoli!

I was nervous at first to try baby-led weaning. If you are too, then start with making your own puréed baby food and store it in glass jars. Most soft foods don't need to be cooked and can be mashed easily with a fork or even just with your baby's hands.

There are great books and guides available to help you on the baby-led weaning journey, and of course, consult your doctor or maternal health nurse before feeding your baby solids.

NAPPIES

Nappies (diapers) make up around 2.5 per cent of landfill, and just thinking about what's inside those nappies is, well, gross, especially when considering it won't break down properly. Much like a disposable sanitary pad, nappies are made of a mix of natural and synthetic (plastic) fibres. Most 'eco' nappies still use plastic, just less of it. Adhesives and dyes also feature prominently on disposable nappies. The production uses a huge amount of non-renewable resources, all for something that is just thrown away after one use – not to mention all the packaging and the plastic bags used for disposal.

The Builder was the one thinking about nappies before I even had. When he asked me if we'd be using reusable nappies, I wondered if it was because he wanted to use disposables. Instead, he gave me a list of the materials found in disposable nappies, declaring he didn't want polyacrylate, polypropylene or any type of bleach near our newborn's skin. He had also told me about a study that showed disposable nappies might affect the sperm count in boys, as they don't allow the skin to breathe properly and raise the temperature of the genitals. Needless to say, The Builder has been right alongside me happily changing our son's nappies and washing them since day one.

If cloth nappies are a struggle, don't feel you've failed. Parenting is hard, especially during the first year. Even just saying no to two disposable nappies a week will save over 100 disposable nappies per year from entering landfill.

Biodegradable and compostable nappies are an option, but unless you can compost them, they still won't break down properly in landfill. There are some companies that sell and then collect compostable nappies for commercial composting.

Modern cloth nappies

Modern cloth nappies (MCNs) are completely different to how things were done with terry towelling nappies thirty years ago. MCNs look like a disposable nappy; the only difference is you don't throw them away. The nappies are kept on with velcro or snaps (no pins), and many brands allow for adjustments in size meaning parents only need to buy one set from birth until toilet training. We were given second-hand MCNs that still worked well; only some of the elastics needed replacing. The main material touching a baby's skin in an MCN is cotton or bamboo.

MCNs are divided into four different styles:

☐ Fitted nappies are the closest in design to a disposable and are usually made using natural fabric, meaning they will require a cover for waterproofing.

☐ All-in-ones do not need an extra cover as the waterproof layer is built in.

☐ All-in-twos have an insert that is snapped into the waterproof cover and removed for washing.

☐ Pocket nappies have an opening between an inner layer and outer waterproof layer to hold an absorbent insert.

Full disclosure, the waterproofing for many MCNs is made of a synthetic material – a thin layer of polyurethane laminate (PUL) – to create the moisture-locking fabric. This stops the nappy from soaking through, which would usually only happen at night for most babies (during the day they are changed more frequently). Instead of using a PUL cover, you can use a wool cover (sometimes called a wool soaker). Wool is anti-bacterial and breaths better than a PUL cover. It is also super absorbent, holding 40 per cent of its own weight in liquid without feeling damp. Washing wool covers in hot water with other nappies will ruin the covers but, unless there has been a major explosion, I simply air out the covers between uses. I then wash and lanolise them once a month using a wool detergent; lanolising helps keep them water resistant.

Fact

Children go through around 6000 nappy changes between birth and toilet training.

Tip

We don't use liners for our nappies (we don't see the point of them), but there are reusable options in cloth, silk and bamboo.

Cloth flats and prefolds

If you would like to go completely plastic-free with nappies, try cloth flats or prefolds. Both are more traditional but still work really well. A flat is a square piece of fabric – cotton terry, flannel, bamboo or a hemp/cotton blend – that is folded into a nappy shape and fastened using a fastener or pin. Flats can be folded in many different ways to suit the shape of the baby. They are the easiest to wash, the fastest to dry and least expensive of all reusable nappy options. If you don't sell them on, they can be up-cycled into cleaning cloths for the house. Prefolds are similar to flats except that they have been sewn into three sections, with the middle one fitted with more layers (with flats you fold them to create this middle section). Flats and prefolds also need a waterproof cover.

Tip

Rather than buy new nappy bins, see if you can take used buckets from a bulk store, pet store or feed store.

Tips for using reusables

A baby in resuables nappies (MCNs, flats or prefolds) will need between twenty-five and thirty nappies, which can be used again for at least two more children. If you are using wool covers, I would invest in three or four of them. On average, we go through six or seven cloth nappies a day (a newborn will start with around twelve per day and gradually slow down).

Cloth nappies take all of fifteen minutes out of our day. They don't require soaking – in fact this can make them less efficient. Instead soiled nappies are washed off into the toilet (we use a hose installed from the hardware store, or you can scrape them down with a knife) then rinsed and put into a nappy bucket or bin. We have three nappy buckets: one sits in our baby's room under the change table, the second is in the laundry and a third comes on any weekend trips away. When out and about, the nappies go into a wash bag. When we have around twelve nappies in a bucket (two days' worth), we will put a load into the washing machine, along with any baby wipes and clothes, using a hot wash and eco-friendly bulk-bought detergent. I also follow the brand's instructions on 'strip washes' (cloth nappy terminology for a deep clean). Australia's warm climate makes reusable nappies easy – they are usually able to dry on the clothesline in the sun, but if it is wet, they are just draped on a clotheshorse inside. Remember, there are cloth-nappy-cleaning services available in most areas for times when you want a break too.

Tip

Anything can be turned into a nappy bag. Ours is an old gym bag we found in the house and carries everything we need. Otherwise look for second-hand options.

Commercial baby wipes often contain irritating ingredients like fragrances. Reusable cloth wipes are soft and will last as long as reusable nappies, so you'll never run out. I recommend purchasing three per reusable nappy just in case. These can be bought online either new or second-hand, and are stored and washed in the same way as the nappies. There are recipes for creating ready-made wet wipes with oils and soap, but we decided to keep it simple and just use water.

I tried to make my own nappy cream but found the end product was not as effective as a store-bought version. Instead, I choose one made by a local naturopath who will take back the glass jars for refill and reuse. Visit a local health food store to see if they stock a locally made version. To minimise the use of nappy cream, I change nappies often and set up nappy-free time during the day to let the area breath. Note when your baby gets a rash – my son is more likely to get a rash when he's teething or ill, or if he or I have consumed something highly acidic. If I suspect it's a rash caused by yeast, I'll dab the area with one part apple-cider vinegar diluted with one part water.

If you are unsure about cloth nappies, look into a cloth nappy library – this allows parents to trial the different types of nappies before making an investment. Parents who use cloth nappies are also usually passionate and willing to share buckets of helpful knowledge, so look for groups online (I've shared some in the Directory, page 265).

Fact

Flushable wipes are sold as degradable but the fibre is tougher than toilet paper. The wipes don't always have time to degrade before they reach the treatment plant, contributing to blockages in sewer mains.

Tip

Instead of a plastic change mat, we bought a bundle of second-hand towels, which are just washed with our nappies.

Modern cloth nappies come in an array of fun patterns and colours.

Cloth flats and wool covers are a completely plastic-free option.

Many of our son's books and toys were mine from when I was younger; others were handed down from family and friends.

We have reusable wipes, along with a glass spray bottle of water and small container of nappy cream, in our nappy bag.

If you are breastfeeding, reusable breast pads will be your new best friends.

Our son is constantly outgrowing his second-hand or handed-down clothes.

yellow

red

Little Golden Book
CLASSIC

The POKY LITTLE PUPPY

RAISING A ZERO-WASTE CHILD

Before our son was even born, we were given so much stuff that we didn't need and that was, ultimately, a waste. For example, our bank sent us stickers and a plastic moneybox when we set up a bank account for him – I returned them immediately saying we needed neither. While we adults are better at saying no to all those marketing trinkets, kids might not be. It might sound difficult to raise a child with zero-waste values in this kind of environment, but see everything as an opportunity to have a conversation about why you avoid waste, and how to say no politely!

I have found discussing zero waste with kids to be less daunting than it sounds. Using activities to help them understand and becoming involved in reducing household waste is a great place to start. Point out and discuss the litter in your neighbourhood. Let them help you do a bin audit or give them the job of looking after the worms in a worm farm. Their little brains are like sponges: involving them in the changes you want to make will not only give them a sense of responsibility but it will also be a way for them to learn and find what works for them. If you'd like to continue the dialogue, I have listed books and movies suitable for children in the Directory (page 260).

As with any lifestyle that is different to the mainstream, it can be rewarding to join groups of like-minded individuals. This is very helpful with zero-waste parenting, not only to see how others are raising children of varying ages but also to see how they have dealt with hiccups. Having a support network of people you can turn to makes the impossible seem possible. The Builder and I have – and know we will continue to – run into further waste-related issues as our son grows, but knowing someone else has gone through and met similar roadblocks in their own journey brings some solidarity.

Having said this, I'm feeling optimistic for the future. Over the past three years I've visited many schools to talk about reducing waste and after each trip, especially to primary schools, I leave wondering why I was invited in the first place, with so many kids already understanding the issues around plastic and our growing landfills and having endless ideas for solutions.

> **Tip**
>
> Ask children for what they want as a gift – it's not wasted if it's something they would play with rather than something eco-friendly that ends up sitting around ignored. The same goes for us big people!

KIDS' PARTIES

I remember when birthday parties consisted of musical chairs and a simple cake. These days, parties seem to be a bit more extravagant, with bins overflowing at the end. A lot of tips for kids' parties are the same as the tips in the Entertaining + Events chapter; for example, looking into electronic invitations. But here are a few more tips to make sure the child still has a great day.

If your child would like a themed party, forget the matching paper cups and instead look into hiring decorations, borrowing from family and friends, or up-cycling. Scraps of fabric can be turned into cloth bunting in place of single-use balloons and streamers. Hold off on the glitter, as most of it is made of plastic that can end up in our waterways. Instead, use leaves, hole-punched paper scraps or cut-out stars from reused paper.

Keep the food simple; since kids are so busy running about with friends, the food is often forgotten anyway! Stuff they can grab easily includes popcorn (which could be made with different flavours), fresh and dried fruit, cupcakes (without the paper cases), and home-made dips and crackers, to name a few. Of course use reusable plates, bowls and cups, and skip the plastic straws.

Look into colouring birthday treats with natural dyes. You only need a splash to add colour, and the flavour won't impact on the cake apart from adding a bit of natural sweetness.

Fact

Balloons easily escape into the environment where they pop, making it easy for wildlife to swallow them or get caught up in the strings.

☐ **red**: beetroot juice

☐ **orange**: carrot juice

☐ **yellow**: a pinch of turmeric dissolved in water

☐ **green**: juice from cooked spinach

☐ **blue**: blueberry juice

☐ **purple**: fresh blackberry juice

Say no to party bags; instead, set aside some cake for the kids to take home. If you'd like to create a carrier, you can fold newspaper into a food box. And ask the kids (or parents) to bring along a reusable container to take home leftover food.

TOYS

Children are curious creatures. Their desire to explore and play appears to know no bounds, so I can understand how the need to constantly supply kids with new toys has become ingrained to the point where we now have rooms in homes dedicated to toys. Most of these inexpensive toys are made of plastic and sold to us as being easily replaceable. During council cleanups I'm always staggered by how many toys have been dumped on the verge when they appear to be in working order.

We put a blanket rule of no new toys in our home except for books, and discussed our decision with family and friends prior to our son's birth. So far, it's been 95 per cent successful. Most fellow parents understand completely, having known themselves the overwhelming amount of toys that seem to flood in with a new child. We can foster our children's curiosity without falling into the need to constantly buy new stuff. One great way is through borrowing. Borrowing also teaches children about sharing and caring for items. Libraries – including school libraries and toy libraries – have great options to keep children entertained, including:

- ☐ puzzles
- ☐ dress ups
- ☐ scooters and bikes
- ☐ musical instruments
- ☐ video and computer games
- ☐ books, of course!

Join dedicated online buy/swap/sell groups to find second-hand toys, or ask family and friends for excess toys they are not using anymore. If buying new toys, look for untreated wooden or food-grade painted toys (local craft markets are often a great source).

Teach your kids the fun of up-cycling through arts and crafts projects, repurposing items found around the house. A cardboard box can be turned into so many things! Be inspired by the different ways your kids can turn 'waste' into something fun and useful. And, when you can, get out of the house – explore museums, zoos and other interactive play areas, or visit local parks and take advantage of play equipment.

Fact

A study by the American Chemical Society in 2011 found that 80 per cent of children's toys were covered in toxic flame-retardants.

Tip

Toy library memberships make great gifts for children, as do other experiences such as zoo or museum passes, art or swimming classes, or a trip to an indoor rock-climbing or laser tag centre.

KIRSTEN MARREN

Wyndham Little Buddies Toy Library

I first joined a toy library when my daughter was six months old. I had heard about it from a friend and the concept of sharing toys just clicked with me. Initially, my motivation was to save on money. At that stage, my baby was changing so rapidly; I could already foresee that toys would be outgrown quickly and the figures would start adding up. And I have to say, that it still so true. My children aren't changing as rapidly as when they were babies, but man, kids get bored of toys fast!

By the end of our first year I realised that another major benefit to the toy library was how it saved so much space – and ultimately saved my sanity. We don't have the luxury of a 'play room' so it didn't take long for me as a new mother to start feeling overwhelmed by the brightly coloured items that seemed to be creeping in all over the house. By rotating toys through our home instead of purchasing them, my house has remained relatively intact.

Going into my second year of membership (and welcoming baby number two) I started to appreciate that the toys weren't mapped out according to 'gender' (pink versus blue) like they were in major retail stores. My daughters roamed the toy library, each choosing their own toys. My eldest has completely different interests to me and loves to build and create. My youngest loves cars and dolls. The diversity of toys allows imaginations to broaden.

It was only in my third year of membership that I looked back on the amount of plastic that hadn't been sent to landfill through the simple act of sharing toys. Our toy library has toys that are twenty years old and still in use, and a great deal of effort goes into mending and repurposing them. And when it comes times for birthdays or Christmas in our house, we usually buy or source toys that have been tried and tested already through the toy library, so we know our children will love and use them over and over.

All toy libraries rely on volunteers to run them, and getting involved through volunteering has been very gratifying, plus I have really enjoyed meeting other new parents in our community. I cannot talk enough about how much I love my toy library.

THE SCHOOL YEARS

As children progress through school there are going to be certain aspects out of your control, unless of course the school has implemented some waste-free concepts. There are a couple of these listed in my Directory (page 260) for inspiration.

Many of the talks I've given at schools have been around 'Nude Food' initiatives. This program encourages children and parents to send lunches to school with less packaging. I have heard comments about how much pressure delivering waste-free lunches at school can be for parents, and I totally understand. Rather than change everything in one go, try changing things slowly. Dedicate one term to sending one less packaged item of food, for example, sandwiches in beeswax wrap or a reusable container. Then follow up in the next term, perhaps by switching juice boxes for reusable water bottles. For helpful tips, look for Facebook groups dedicated to families reducing their waste and swap stories. Less packaging often leads to healthier eating habits.

I can proudly say that I had the same lunchbox from primary school through to the end of high school. But a friend who is a teacher recently told me that kids at her school often go through many different lunchboxes in one school year! Lunchboxes made of stainless steel have less chance of breaking and, if cared for, will last all the years at school. Some schools have school-assigned backpacks that will be held onto for the duration of a child's time at the school, and many school backpacks come with a warranty.

School stationery can also be wasteful as kids feel the need to upgrade every year, but most items apart from notebooks can be bought to last if they are cared for. Some teachers end up with a surplus of items left over at the end of each term or year, so it could be worth checking with them to see what can be salvaged and reused. Instead of spiral notebooks with plastic covers, opt for regular stapled notebooks – the less complex the material makeup of items, the easier they are to recycle.

Tip

Second-hand uniforms are readily available, otherwise buy one size larger than needed and hem pants or skirts.

Tip

Instead of covering textbooks in plastic contact paper, protect them for resale with brown paper.

FURRY FRIENDS

If you are interested in bringing a pet into your life, consider how they could reduce waste for you. Chickens are a great option as they eat most vegetable food scraps from the home and, in return, you get eggs and chicken poo for fertiliser. There are many animals looking for a home, so make sure you visit an animal shelter. Adopting a pet will bring a lot of joy to your life and to theirs too!

Dedicated online groups for different pets are a good place to seek out second-hand shelters like kennel boxes, rabbit cages and beds for indoor pets. You could even look at making your own up-cycled enclosures. Like children, pets don't mind second-hand toys to chew or chase. If you do want to buy new, look for toys made of natural fibres such as cotton, wool or hemp, so they'll break down without polluting the environment. You can also find second-hand food and water bowls; otherwise look for sturdy stainless steel.

Cats naturally clean themselves, but dogs require a bath from time to time. Look for unpackaged, dog-friendly shampoo bars online or by contacting local soap-makers. Keep fleas at bay without the packaged chemical repellents by regularly vacuuming your home, as well as lots of shampooing and grooming using a brush or flea comb. Fleas are put off by the smells of rosemary, lavender, cedar, citronella, mint and citrus. A common natural flea repellent is to boil lemon rind covered with water in a saucepan. Simmer on low for 20 minutes, then cool, strain and transfer to a glass spray bottle. Work into your dog's coat and brush through. Feeding a small amount of brewer's yeast to cats and dogs can also turn fleas off.

Tip

Bones can be picked up packaging-free from butchers for dogs to chew on.

Tip

Regular outdoor airing and a sprinkling of bicarb soda (baking soda) on a pet bed will help reduce any smell.

Local pet stores may sell pet food in bulk – there are even some dedicated bulk stores for pet food. Otherwise, opt to buy the largest bag of food possible and recycle the plastic packaging through a soft-plastics recycling program. You could also try making your own pet food. There are many recipes available and most items, including vegetables, meat and grains, can be purchased package-free. If you do plan on making your own pet food, it is best to consult with a your vet to make sure your animals receive the nutrients needed to stay healthy. They might even have some recipes to share with you.

> **Tip**
>
> Rabbit or guinea pig poo can be used directly in the garden as a natural fertiliser.

> **Tip**
>
> My research has found flushing both dog and cat poo down the toilet to be unsafe. However, contact your local wastewater treatment facility or local council to verify this for your region.

There are other solutions to deal with dog poo rather than tossing it into landfill in plastic bags. While biodegradable bags are sold as the 'smarter' way to pick up dog waste when out walking or around the house, there are other options like newspaper, paper bags or a reusable poo scooper. Biodegradable bags *are* a smarter choice than plastic, but they don't always break down, especially in landfill where the conditions are not right, plus they encourage the single-use mentality. When dog poo is thrown into a normal landfill bin, the waste itself also won't break down properly. While you shouldn't add pet poo to your normal compost, there are dedicated pet composts available.

For kitty litter, use dirt or sawdust, or look for brands selling walnut shells – you'll be giving what would be a wasted by-product of walnut production another use. The walnut shells can be used for other pets such as birds and reptiles.

> **Fact**
>
> If you pick up after your dog three times a day using plastic bags, this puts 1095 plastic bags into landfill each year.

AMANDA CHAPMAN

wastefreeland.nz

I live in central Auckland, New Zealand, and have been living waste-free for several years. My favourite thing about it has been getting to know the local community members that I would not have met had I continued doing my grocery shopping at large supermarket chains.

I have a 10-year-old cat who is very low maintenance and self-sufficient. It's fairly easy to stay low-waste with a cat, especially one that is in good health.

I feed my cat dry biscuits as he prefers them. I buy them either from a bulk bin package-free, or in a very large bulk size. My cat also eats eggs and any leftover meat from my flatmates (with chicken being his favourite). I encourage hunting of rats and mice (but not birds!).

My cat hates using a litter tray and, instead, goes to the toilet outside. You can buy biodegradable litter; however, it's not advisable to compost it due to the risk of toxoplasmosis, which is a disease that can be transferred by a parasite found in cat faeces. It's most harmful to pregnant women, young children and people with weak immune systems.

PET ACCESSORIES

☐ Cat toys are easy to make and kittens love playing with simple things like toilet rolls or balls. My cat's favourite game is chasing shadows and lights, which is as simple and low waste as you can get! I also bought hand-knitted mice from my local second-hand store.

☐ Originally, I bought a cat bed, but I soon found that my cat preferred to sleep anywhere but there. I donated the bed and now don't bother with any fancy bedding. My cat's favourite spot is on the windowsill, which is wide enough for him to lie on while also keeping guard.

☐ I brush my cat using an old hairbrush. I usually let the fur blow away (as I brush him outside), or it can be composted.

☐ Instead of plastic collars, I buy natural ones made from cotton, hemp or soy. My cat has gone through a few collars and he's micro chipped, so he actually doesn't wear one anymore. When he was younger, he always wore a collar and bell to scare birds, but now he's too slow for them and prefers to catch rats anyway.

PET HEALTH

☐ I have a longhaired cat, so fleas are a common problem. I buy flea treatments that generate recyclable and non-recyclable waste.

☐ To kill carpet fleas, I use food-grade diatomaceous earth (DE) powder purchased from a bulk store. To use, just sprinkle it on the carpet and vacuum up, or brush it into your pet's fur. Please be careful that you and your pet do not inhale the powder.

☐ Worm tablets can be purchased as needed from your local vet or pet store. They usually put these in a small resealable plastic bag. You can either reuse this bag, or take a small jar or paper envelope to carry the pill home in.

☐ Medical waste is a given. My cat is not often sick, but if he is I won't deprive him of necessary medications due to waste.

LITTLE PEOPLE + FURRY FRIENDS TOP TIPS

CHANGE ONE THING

Buy second-hand clothes for children over brand new.
They will likely grow out of them very soon anyway!

CHANGE TWO THINGS

Look to purchase pet food in bulk – your local pet
shop might have an option. Otherwise, buy the
biggest bag you can and recycle the soft plastic.

CHANGE THE WORLD

If you've got a little person in your life, cloth nappies
and reusable cloth wipes are two of the biggest
changes that you can make to reduce waste.
Even just saying no to two disposable nappies
a week will save 104 disposable nappies per year
from entering landfill.

PART THREE

TRICKS

ON THE ROAD

I am an avid traveller locally and abroad – in fact, The Rogue Ginger originally started as a travel blog. I thrill at the thought of stepping beyond my backyard, exploring unfamiliar towns, states and countries; trying new foods; immersing myself in other cultures, histories and languages. Humans' love of travel has never diminished through the centuries, and advancements in technology have made travel easier and more affordable.

Being in a new location has the potential to disrupt established patterns of low-waste habits. Reducing waste outside the house – whether it's travelling overseas or simply being at our workplaces and social events – can be a challenge, but I can assure you, many of the habits learned through this book can be taken with you and also inspire change in others.

Tip

Zero Waste App is an amazing resource to locate grocers and bulk stores, cafes and restaurants, farmers' markets, composting locations, water refill stations and zero-waste groups across the world.

EATING ON THE GO

If you're going on a road trip or just to a one-day festival, try to take snacks so you're not tempted by over-packaged fast food, or plan ahead for a sit-down lunch. Before sitting down in a cafe or restaurant, look around at the meals people are having and don't be afraid to ask some questions about how things are served, like salad dressing in a small plastic container or straws in drinks.

Staying in to cook while travelling can reduce waste and save you money. If I'm staying in self-contained accommodation for longer than a couple of days, I like to ask them what they have in their kitchen; for instance, if they don't have a tea strainer, I will take my own. If you're driving and know there will be no bulk shopping options at your destination, pack some basic supplies in the car to take with you.

While cooking where you stay is fun, going out to restaurants, bars and cafes is part of the experience of travelling. I'm a big believer that eating local food is one of the best ways to get to know a country. Local city markets or farmers' markets were a fun tourist experience for me long before I went zero waste. You get to try some of the best and freshest food, while also supporting small businesses. As well as fruit and nuts to snack on, or ingredients to cook with if you are staying somewhere with a kitchen, you can also find some great takeaway food options at markets and, of course that doesn't have to mean waste. I've yet to be turned down at a market when asking (in various languages) to have something in my own container.

There are several options to take care of food scraps while out of the house, depending on location. If you're not far from home, collect and carry your compost to take with you. Dumping leftover food in a park might seem like a good solution but it risks attracting animals to unwanted areas. ShareWaste.com allows you to find someone in the area you're in who's willing to accept extra food waste and compost it. Community gardens are another way to compost food scraps while travelling. If none of these options are available try, cutting up the food scraps into small pieces and burying them at a depth animals would find hard to reach.

YOUR WASTE NOT KIT

Whether you're on a long trip or out for the day, be prepared for eating and drinking on the go.

- A tea towel (dish towel) has multiple purposes, from drying your reusables to wrapping food up or becoming a makeshift picnic seat.

- Cloth bags can be used to collect plastic-free produce or snack food at a market.

- Picnic plates and bowls aren't just for picnics – use them to pick up takeaway food from a market stall or roadside diner.

- A cup or jar comes in handy for holding snacks in the car, grabbing a coffee to go, or storing food scraps for composting. My personal favourite use is collecting scoops of ice cream if the store doesn't have cones.

- My cutlery wrap (see the DIY on page 230) neatly holds my cutlery, serviette, chopsticks and reusable straw.

Tip

Plastic bottled water is not the only way to avoid unsafe drinking water. Boiling clear water is the safest way to kill bacteria. I boil water for five minutes before letting the water cool before drinking. Another option is a reusable water purification system.

Tip

Bring your own coffee and tea to avoid the single-use packets in hotel rooms and guesthouses. You can either compost the tea and coffee, or sprinkle it around a plant.

CUTLERY WRAP

My hand-made cutlery wrap, sewn together from scrap fabric, has started many conversations around the use of plastic utensils, especially on flights. (I prefer to keep wooden cutlery in my cutlery wrap as it's less likely to be removed on international flights.) Make the wrap and the pockets whatever size you need to fit your utensils. If you are not a keen sewer check online for pre-made options, up-cycle an old pencil case, or wrap utensils in a tea towel (dish towel) with an elastic band or ribbon.

TRAVEL

Thinking of travel, images of fuel-guzzling airplanes or cars might spring to mind – not very zero waste. But, with our desire to connect, see and explore, I can't ever imagine people will stop travelling. Instead, we can make choices to do so sustainably as we navigate across this beautiful earth.

Ecotourism is the practice of being responsible and sustainable with our travel choices: leaving no trace, preserving resources, choosing not to disturb ecosystems, spending our money so it may have a social benefit and, of course, reducing our waste. Travelling with this mindset allows us to connect with not only the location but also the culture and local people more authentically, and to enjoy respectful and meaningful adventures.

Airline recycling and waste management is made difficult for two reasons: the varying quarantine laws in different countries and airports lacking the facilities to deal with waste materials. This is an ongoing area being investigated by airlines and airports around the world. In the meantime, carry your own earplugs, headphones, toiletries and a scarf (to use as a blanket or pillow) so that you can refuse the plastic-wrapped options on the plane. Don't be afraid to cancel your meal and, instead, take your own food with you on the flight – I like to take vegetable sticks, fresh fruit and sandwiches. (Some countries have strict quarantine laws, so check what food you can bring or make sure you eat everything you bring while you're on the plane.) And always opt for electronic tickets if available.

It can be a minefield looking for accommodation with sustainable values aligned with your own. There are eco-retreats, eco-hotels and eco-lodges boasting energy- and water-saving measures and proper waste systems to divert as much from landfill as possible. But, unfortunately, 'eco' can be slapped onto anything without meeting any credentials. The perfect zero-waste accommodation is going to be hard to find, but you can still reduce your footprint by choosing homestays or couch surfing, camping, housesitting, small guesthouses and bed and breakfasts. These consume less water and energy than larger resorts and hotels and are more likely to have vegetable gardens and composting options, as well as offering you more connections to the local community.

Tip

Many flights will not allow passengers to bring full water bottles (reusable or disposable) onto the plane. Once onboard the plane, ask the flight attendants to fill your empty bottle.

Fact

In 2010, Green America found the average airline passenger created 500 grams of waste per flight. With the number of flights ever increasing, that's a lot of rubbish.

The internet has made it so easy to connect with like-minded people on your travels. Look for the same local resources you would in your own area, such as zero-waste or plastic-free groups and bloggers, to find helpful information on where you are going, and don't be afraid to ask questions. Before I travelled to Myanmar, China and the Philippines, I asked local environmental groups I found on the internet to help translate phrases like 'no plastic straw, please'. This may not always work, but trying is better than not. Plus, you get to learn some words in a new language! You could also email queries to the local town information centre or to your accommodation; they could pass on information such as recycling locations, bike hire or how to access clean drinking water without having to buy plastic bottles.

Finally, have fun, and don't feel too bad if some things don't go to plan – that's what travel is all about!

TO SOUVENIR OR NOT TO SOUVENIR

Collecting tokens to keep or to give as gifts is a favourite pastime for many travellers. I can be sentimental when it comes to holidays, but that doesn't mean that I collect gimmicky plastic items. Many of my souvenirs are clothing pieces I've purchased from second-hand stores or fair-trade local makers – it's nice putting something on that brings back memories of trips to Nova Scotia, Cambodia or Estonia. If you are partial to a physical item, seek out fair-trade and ethical stores and markets where you can meet the maker and learn something along to the way. Make sure you think about whether you'll actually wear or use something when you get home!

Instead of a physical souvenir, perhaps opt to spend more on a meaningful experience. For example, when I went travelling through Eastern Europe with my brother, we didn't have much money but we kept some aside so that at each visit to a country we could indulge in a fancy meal. Your own souvenir experience could be anything.

The Builder and I do have a strict rule of no souvenirs for anyone but ourselves, purely because too much time is spent trying to find that right something for someone who we're never absolutely sure will love it anyway. Instead, we might choose to send a postcard to family and friends.

Tip

Look to see what you can hire or borrow from friends before adventuring. Items like tents, eskys, sleeping bags and folding chairs can all be borrowed rather than bought brand new.

Tip

If your accommodation toiletries look like they have been used at all, the cleaning crew is likely to throw them away. Instead, bring your own and take the complimentary ones to the front desk or leave a note saying you didn't use any.

PACKING

Choosing to travel with just carry-on luggage not only reduces fuel consumption in cars or planes (which increases with weight). It will also avoid the need for checked baggage labels, which are usually not recyclable and are printed on BPA-coated stickers. Plus, it frees up time spent waiting for the luggage at the carousel!

The key to packing carry-on is to roll clothes and place them into bags with similar items (such as tops and bottoms in one bag, underwear and pyjamas in another). This method is helpful if you are trying to find items quickly, like at five in the morning in a fifteen-person dorm room on the top floor of a dark hostel in Prague while trying not to wake anyone up. My usual rule is:

Tip

I keep little bottles that I've collected over the years to decant small amounts of oils and tooth powder so I can stay fresh on long-haul flights.

- ☐ 2 x tops
- ☐ 2 x bottoms
- ☐ 1 x skirt
- ☐ 5 x underwear
- ☐ 2 x bras
- ☐ 2 x shoes

- ☐ 2 x socks
- ☐ 1 x swimsuit
- ☐ 1 x pyjamas
- ☐ 1 x jacket that can double as a rain jacket
- ☐ limited accessories

Shoes are a good place to pack socks into if space is tight. I also pack an extra bar of soap among my clothes to keep them smelling fresh.

While packing, write a list of the possible parts of your trip where you'll make waste and consider a solution. For example, most hotel laundry services will return clothes individually wrapped in plastic or in a plastic bag. Instead, provide a cloth bag (the same one you're packing your clothes into, perhaps) or wash clothes in your room using soap brought from home. Make sure to pack clothing in fabrics that wash and dry easily.

Tip

Up-cycle your old plastic shower cap to use as shoe protectors when you are packing.

Make sure the cutlery wrap in your *Waste Not* kit includes wooden cutlery if you're getting on a plane.

Always pack your reusable drink bottle.

Guides, maps and apps can help to find food markets and water fountains, or translate useful phrases.

Pack your clothes in separate bags, which can also be used as laundry bags.

Mini toiletries mean you can avoid the complimentary disposables supplied by accommodation and planes.

I always carry a clothesline so I can wash clothes in my accommodation – the soap for washing also keeps clothes smelling fresh.

A hanky is great for unexpected colds, carrying food and cleaning.

Earplugs, headphones and scarf will allow you to say no to plastic-wrapped options on the plane.

SISKA NIRMALA PUSPITASARI

Adventure enthusiast and journalist
zerowasteadventures.com

Waking up one fine morning, in the midst of pine forests, on a peaceful camping trip with a friend and his five-year-old son – the small boy stood with a tiny box of milk in his hand. I looked at him and smiled, but then he started to cry – because he was scared I would be mad because he had produced trash. A couple of months later, we all went camping again together. This time my friend brought another milk alternative for his son: a can of condensed milk, which is easier to recycle.

I live in Bandung, West Java province, Indonesia. I'm a journalist, and an adventure enthusiast. Adventuring is a growing trend in Indonesia, especially among the younger generations. My awareness of the trash problem started with my adventures, as the increase in adventure tourism has led to more waste. I have adopted a zero-waste lifestyle since 2012, and have run zero-waste expeditions to five mountains in Indonesia. These life-changing experiences have altered my paradigm about why reducing waste in the first place is very important, and have also allowed me to advocate a zero-waste lifestyle to the younger generations here in Indonesia.

Every time I go for an adventure, whether it's backpacking, hiking or just camping with some friends, I never force others to prepare and pack everything as zero-waste as can be. But they try to pack less waste by themselves – first, because they feel ashamed with me, but then because they feel happy to reduce their own waste while we're on our adventure. This is why I believe adventures are more than just an activity. Adventures are a statement.

TIPS FOR ZERO-WASTE ADVENTURING

☐ Preparing the details is the most important thing to achieve your zero-waste goals during the adventure. Of course basic zero-waste essentials like reusable bottles, food containers and cloth bags are a must. But to go mountain hiking somewhere like Indonesia, for example, you'll need more specific preparation to be able to cope with the tropical weather.

☐ I recommend using a cooking set with an alcohol stove. It's better than using a gas stove, which needs disposable canned gas. Canned gas is one of the most widely found rubbish items at Indonesian mountains, after disposable bottles.

☐ Consider staying at a local hostel rather than a hotel. It gives you many benefits, especially to support your mission in reducing waste. Of course, it also supports the local economy and small businesses. You can easily refill your reusable bottle, get great local food and wisdom, and there are no excessive facilities that you don't actually need. And the most important thing in Indonesia is that these hostels cherish the groundwater – the biggest problem of Indonesian tourism is the water used by all the new hotels, causing drought for the local residents. Many online platforms nowadays make it easy to find hostels.

☐ Experiencing the local food is one thing that must be on your travelling bucket list. There are many great local Indonesian foods, and you should buy them at the local vendors. Bringing your own container is the easiest way to take away food. But it can't be denied: sometimes you'll find a tricky food vendor who refuses a special order like yours, perhaps because they are very busy or don't understand. You just need a simple trick to prevent this from happening: order food to dine in, and then, when it is served on plates, transfer it to your food container.

☐ If you decide to use a mountain guide or porter for an adventure, do your own preparation or educate them about how to reduce waste, as they may have a lack of environmental awareness.

WORKPLACES

Getting out of the house doesn't just mean going on a big trip. We spend over 30 per cent of our lives at our workplaces. It's here we interact with a variety of people on a professional level, some with shared ideals and some with whom we have nothing in common. Up until the birth of my son, I worked regular 9–5 corporate jobs. None of them were ever related to the environment, except for one advertising pitch for a city park sign redesign – that was as close as it got.

What can you do working in an office full of people who don't share the same outlook as you? While it could be tempting to stand on your desk and give an impassioned speech about reducing waste, leading by example is always one of the kindest – and most effective – ways to enact change. Since the office is a place where we spend so much of our time, having extra reusables by our side will help reduce waste when we pop out for a morning coffee or lunch. I kept a reusable takeaway container in the drawer of my office desk to avoid single-use plastic takeaway containers if I hadn't brought my lunch from home. Reaching for your reusable coffee mug or pulling out a sandwich in beeswax wrap can act as a conversation starter about your journey in cutting down rubbish.

You might find other allies in your office sooner than you think. Who knows, you could encourage a closet environmentalist who has been too nervous about proclaiming that everyone should print double sided! There might be the odd person who will provide a bit of push back; just smile, thank them for their views and move on.

> **Tip**
>
> If you don't have a compost set up at work, use a plastic container to collect your own food waste to take home each day, or store it in the work freezer to take home on a regular basis (just make sure to write a note so no one tries to eat it!).

> **Tip**
>
> Suggest that your office purchase items like tea, coffee, sugar and dish-washing liquid in bulk.

Soon, you might be the go-to person in the office to help advise on any type of sustainable change. As your confidence grows, you could think about suggesting steps for the whole company to move forward with low-waste changes. This is obviously easier if you are already in a managerial position, or if you work for yourself. However, these days it is not uncommon for a business to take some action on eco-initiatives. People are recognising that customers respect a company for doing something good, so don't be afraid to start speaking up! You could even pull together a sustainability team in the office. Some companies run team-building days – suggest getting involved with a local clean-up as a way of starting conversations.

Setting up an audit of the waste created by the company (refer back to the bin audit in Part One, page 46) is a great step to foster change and to get people thinking about your office bins. Are there designated signs to point out recycling? Perhaps a compost bin in the kitchen would reduce waste. Instead of having a single bin under each desk, sharing bins might also help with accountability for what is being thrown away. Plus, it gives everyone an excuse to get up and stretch those legs and arms.

The tips included in this section could be applicable in other communities you are part of as well, including schools or sporting clubs, as well as your own home.

Fact

The US Environmental Protection Agency reported in 2008 that 16 per cent of landfill waste was comprised of paper, with much of that being computer printouts, copying and notepads from offices or schools.

Tip

Changing your font can save you ink! Ryman Eco is a sustainable (and beautiful) font designed to save 33 per cent more ink than the office go-to font Times New Roman. Plus it is free to download.

PAPER AND PRINTING – OR NOT

Instead of printing off documents to share or mark up changes, why not do it all digitally? This will save not only reams of paper but also money and space in your office. Look up online tutorials for adding comments and corrections in the programs you use.

There are also countless options these days to automate pay cheques and leave forms as emails, which are easily accessible should they need to be tracked down in the future rather than hunting through old printed files. Opting for electronic power bills, bank statements and receipts is another way to reduce the paper consumed in an office (and at home). Even taxes can be done online, with most information saved from last year, meaning you can save time doing them next year as well as saving paper.

While sticky notes do come in a variety of colours to suit your space and mood, remember there are other waste-saving alternatives. Envelopes, the bottom of a letter, or an old print-off can be used to write to-do lists or jot down that phone number. Cut or tear them to size and put them in a spot on your desk within easy reach, perhaps bound with a bulldog clip. Scrap paper also has a number of other uses – including being perfect drawing paper for kids – before it's recycled or composted.

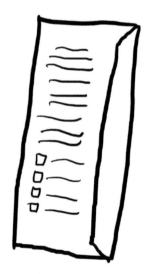

Tip

Remove the plastic window from the envelopes to recycle with soft plastics before using the envelope for notes and shopping lists.

If you're switching to digital documents, make sure that you have a good digital filing system so that everything is still easily located. If your office requires you to file hardcopy documents in binder folders, try to regularly empty files that are no longer needed so that the folders can be reused (making sure to recycle the paper). Alternatively, look out for recycled cardboard binders without the plastic wrap.

Many businesses like to send out catalogues, stationery or other marketing material – most of this could be sent electronically, or not at all, as much goes unread. Opting for electronic can help reduce plastic usage as well as paper, since catalogues often come wrapped in a soft-plastic bag that can only be down-cycled. If you like reading catalogues but do not want to sacrifice an acre of woodland, see if they can be accessed digitally.

If you do need to print, try to use recycled paper. One tonne of recycled paper could save up to seventeen virgin trees. Look on the paper packaging to make sure it is from post-consumer paper and if in doubt call the manufacturer hotline. Don't forget to look for Totally Chlorine Free (TCF) or Processed Chlorine Free (PCF) paper too. Printing on both sides will also reduce waste, as will only printing in black and white – colour printing means more printer cartridges will need to be refilled. And make sure that you *are* refilling your printer cartridges, instead of just purchasing new ones – you will save on packaging, plastic and money.

Tip

Look into cancelling the paper phone directory book sent out each year; instead look up phone numbers in an online directory.

Tip

If you are moving into an empty workspace, skip the trip to Ikea and fill your new space with second-hand furniture bought at second-hand stores or online – you'll save money and find interesting individual pieces.

STATIONERY

Refill pens are not a new concept. The inexpensive pens we use today have only been around since the late 1940s; prior to that, people wrote with pens that were refilled. These still exist and are worth the investment. Offices go through so many pens, with the usual reason being that the ink has become dry or simply run out. The whole pen is thrown away when really only one item needs replacing: the cartridge.

You can also find refillable whiteboard and drawing markers. Don't forget non-toxic pencils are a great option too. Before I left the office each day, I would look over my to-do list and highlight the jobs that required queries from clients or needed urgent attention. These days, I use highlighter pencils instead. They're plastic-free and don't run out of ink – all they require is a sharpener (and the sharpenings can be composted).

Finally, when it comes to stationary, consider what you really need. Most of the identical items sitting in everyone's drawers could be shared around the office instead of being bought new again and again. This includes staplers, tape dispensers and hole punchers.

> **Tip**
>
> If you keep your eyes peeled you'll come across pens discarded all over the place. I found one washed up on a beach two years ago and am still using it.

JONATHAN LEVY

Zero-waste business associate
zerowasteguy.com

I live and breathe all things zero waste, and I am fortunate to be able to say that I work in sustainability too, which means I can practice what I preach.

I am an environmental consultant, working with businesses in Los Angeles on waste reduction and recycling strategies. This usually starts by conducting a waste characterisation where I separate and weigh all the materials generated at a business by type: trash, recycling or organics. This allows me to calculate the percentage of the materials that are recyclable or compostable. It also makes for a great visual aid for the customer, since they can see not only what percentage of their material can be diverted from a landfill, but also how good they are at putting the right materials in the right containers.

From there, I make suggestions for ways in which the client can reduce waste. For some businesses, this means adding recycling programs where none existed before. For others, it means helping them reduce the volume and mass of waste produced by identifying disposable items that can be switched out for reusables. Or, most importantly, it means reducing the production of excess materials (food, manufacturing by-products, etc.), which is better known as 'Source Reduction'. Hey, if you don't create and consume it, you don't have to worry about what happens to it after you throw it 'away', wherever that is!

An example of a great zero-waste win was at a busy jewellery retailer I was working with. They had eight huge trash bins that were emptied six days per week, but no recycle bins. After completing a visual inspection of their material I determined that at least half of it was recyclable. Overnight they went from eight trash bins to four while adding four recycle bins by separating just two items: cardboard and small paperboard jewellery boxes. And, since they were taking the trouble of separating their cardboard, they started selling it, creating a new revenue stream.

My goal, of course, is to zero waste the heck out of every business I work with. In reality, though, that's not always possible. Moving the needle in the right direction is painstakingly slow and, often, frustrating. Since there will always be more waste to divert from landfills, I must not forget to celebrate the small victories.

ACT YOUR VISION

It's the action, not the fruit of the action, that's important. You have to do the right thing. It may not be in your power, may not be in your time, that there'll be any fruit. But that doesn't mean you stop doing the right thing. You may never know what results come from your action. But if you do nothing, there will be no result.

– Mahatma Gandhi

The word activism can be polarising. You might picture people chaining themselves to trees or marching through streets, placards above heads, shouting chants. I remember doing an interview with a radio station and the host introduced me as an activist. It felt like such an extreme description and I left feeling embarrassed and afraid of what people would think of me. I couldn't shake the feeling for days, until The Builder, in his wisdom, told me I *was* an activist – because I was acting my vision. From then on, I redefined what activism was and how I saw it. For me, activism is about living in alignment with how you would like to see the world: choosing kindness, living with intention and taking responsibility.

Activism is not confined to rallies and controversial gestures. Activism is seen in everyday choices: in how and where we spend our money, the people we support, the conversations we have, and what we do to lead by example. These choices will create the vision we want for the future. Saying no to plastic bags or returning a plastic straw to the waiter who forgot to leave it out of your drink makes you an everyday activist. Repairing and up-cycling is a form of activism. Sharing a photo or article with family and friends on reducing waste is activism, since you are helping to raise awareness. Writing this book is a form of activism. Writing a letter to your local representative is activism. Sending wasteful packaging or items back to the company, asking them to design more intelligently, is activism. There are many different levels of activism and they all count. Each one fuels the movement and sends a message asking for a new way, a new system.

Activism in all its form is important because it creates a dialogue for change. But this goes beyond just sharing your journey with the people you encounter and leading by example. Humans are good at coming together and working for a unified cause. The fastest way

Tip

Picking up rubbish is a really simple and visible way to lead by example: all you need are two hands and five minutes! You might think people will judge you, but it's more likely that they will think you're an awesome human, and you'll probably influence someone to do the same.

we will ever reduce the amount of waste entering our environment is to demand legislation to halt the problem before it begins. This helps move some of the responsibility off our shoulders, as consumers, where it has been sitting for too long. We can't only buy our way out of this, nor should we constantly have to pick up other people's rubbish. If you've thought about starting up a campaign in your city or town, get started and go! There is no better time.

Activism might still sound daunting. You might not feel like you are up to it. You might believe that it's all too hard and that the problems are too big. But our oceans are filling up with plastic and landfills are expanding across the world. We need to stop robbing people of their right to clean and safe working conditions, and we need to preserve the earth's resources for something other than a very unnecessary plastic straw. Humans have to remember we are not only consumers but citizens.

WRITE A LETTER

I have sent many letters and emails to businesses and government representatives. A personalised letter shows the time that went into physically putting it together. Letters don't have to be lengthy or full of statistics citing the ending of the world. I form my letters by starting with who I am and then outline the issue. I'll then use bullet points to highlight ways to make changes going forward. I try to stick to one subject and not make my message too complicated.

I've never expected a response; my goal is to simply alert a company or government to the possibility of redesigning an item or system, why it's necessary for change to come about and why it would benefit everyone. It might leave a deflating feeling to not receive a response or to see no immediate action, but your words may still prompt someone somewhere to do more research and set the foundations for change.

Fact

UK restaurant chain Pizza Express committed to stop handing out plastic straws after receiving a letter from a five-year-old girl explaining that plastic straws are bad for animals, often getting stuck in their noses and mouths. This will stop 1.8 million plastic straws from being used each year by its London restaurants alone.

SEND IT BACK

I always encourage people to send back items to companies if they have poorly designed packaging or can't be recycled or fixed. Here is an example of a letter I sent to a company last year for medical blister packs. I always begin a letter or email with a friendly opening, highlighting the product I'm writing to them about, and follow up with an idea on how they could redesign the product or packaging to be less wasteful. I might also include some facts as to why this change is so important. I sign off with my name and contact address (just in case they get in touch to thank me for coming up with the idea for their fantastic new low-waste packaging!).

Dear product managers,

I am sending part of your packaging back, as I could not find a way to dispose of it, other than to landfill. As a consumer, it should not be my full responsibility to figure out if packaging like your blister packs can be recycled. I believe you could do better.

I have included a sample of how you could make a simple swap from the plastic and aluminium blister pack to full aluminium. This would make your pill packets 100 per cent recyclable. The swap would keep blister packs out of landfill, reduce resources and ensure that the next generation will not have to deal with our rubbish. Plastic production and its use can be harmful, and landfills across the world are expanding due to poor packaging designs like this.

I hope you will consider switching to full aluminium blister packs.

Sincerely,

Erin Rhoads

HOST AN EVENT

Host a talk or workshop in your home, school, workplace or through a local community group on simple ways to reduce rubbish. Invite a blogger to present, or do it yourself! A PowerPoint mixed with some courage could influence change in more people than you'll realise. If you have mending skills, help others learn the basics. Op shop like it's your job? Try organising a tour in your area to show people your secrets. I still get jittery before I do a talk but over the years I've learnt audiences big and small like to listen to passionate people with real stories, and yours just might have the potential to inspire someone to grow tomatoes, up-cycle that broken chair or cook the most amazing dish with leftovers.

SIGN ONLINE

I know there are legions of people out there who see online activism as a half-hearted form of activism. I disagree. Since we all have varying levels of ability to get involved, the online world might be where someone feels they can share their views safely while making an impact. The online world has given people a platform to express and explore their views on reducing waste and to find solidarity with others.

Online activism through blogs, social media, apps and websites has helped bolster the zero-waste message, giving urgent light to this social issue. Online petitions do raise awareness – and they can do so quickly. The internet has given us a direct line of communication with businesses and our elected political leaders, and the visibility of comments shared allows others to join the conversation. You only need look through the number of local zero-waste groups set up on Facebook to see the power of conversations happening online. It's through these social channels that we are able to find out where and how we might want to participate in different levels of activism.

> ### Fact
> Anita Horan began her online campaign against over-packaged fruit and vegetables in supermarkets with the hashtag #plasticfreeproduce. The conversations created through this simple hashtag have now gone worldwide.

HOST A MOVIE NIGHT

There are many wonderful movies dedicated to the topic of reducing plastic and waste. If you have been inspired to share the message in a fun and engaging way, I suggest hosting a movie night in your community.

☐ Choose a movie. There are some great suggestions in the Directory (page 262); some of my favourites include *The Clean Bin Project*, *A Plastic Ocean* and *Bag It*. Check the screening licence – this ensures the people who worked on the film are fairly paid. The licence fee will be determined by factors like the size of the event and if it's free or ticketed.

☐ Locate a place to host the screening. This could be a community centre or library using a projector screen, or a cinema. Choosing a venue first will help you gauge what numbers you can have at your movie night.

☐ While free movie nights are great, sometimes setting a price for tickets will guarantee people will turn up. The cost could be just enough to cover your fees, or the proceeds could be donated to a local environmental community group.

☐ Use an online ticketing system to keep things easy, and allow door sales as well just in case some people turn up without a ticket.

☐ Challenge friends and family to bring along a certain number of guests to help spread the message.

☐ If you need sponsors to cover the cost don't be afraid to ask. These could be bookstores, cafes, restaurants or bulk stores. They might even donate some low-waste food for your guests to snack on, or items to use in a raffle that could help to cover costs or raise money.

☐ You might want to organise a speaker or host a panel discussion around the theme of the movie.

☐ Contact local radio stations, newspapers or online community directories to help market the event for you. Use social media to set up the event so it can be shared around easily.

☐ If you want to create a movie feel, pop some popcorn or encourage your guests to bring along low-waste snacks.

JOIN OR START A GROUP

There are so many groups across the world engaging in a range of activities, acting the vision they would like to see for their communities. Sometimes joining a big eco-organisation can be difficult and make you feel like you're not having an impact, whereas smaller community groups usually engage in simple, achievable actions with results you can really see. Use an internet search or ask in a Facebook group to find one that you would like to work with. Here are a couple of my favourites.

Boomerang Bags is a community-driven initiative bringing together individuals with varying skills to make reuseable bags using recycled and donated materials. The bags are left at stores in the community for people who forget their reusable bags. People are encouraged to bring the bags back when they return to the store for someone else to use. What I love about Boomerang Bags is that it creates a helpful item while sharing a message at the same time. Presently, there are over 500 groups around the world and anyone can start one up in their area.

Operation Straw is a Sydney-based group that is combining litter collection and data collection to help spark change. Every Saturday, local divers and snorkellers come together to collect straws littered in a specific area in Manly Cove. The straws are then sorted and the data is recorded, making note of the tides and weather conditions in the week of the collection to help figure out why plastic straws are ending up in the cove and where they could be coming from. In nine weeks the group of volunteers gathered over 1500 plastic straws. This simple exercise will undoubtedly be important in helping to bring about a potential change in the law or business practices in the community. Operation Straw has been featured on national news, allowing its message to reach and inspire many people – who knows where else a similar initiative might now pop up!

If you can't find a group in your area and would like to go beyond engaging online, then you might consider starting your own group. Here are some tips on getting a group together to rally collectively on an issue.

☐ Set out a clear and achievable goal or intention for the group.

☐ Choose a group name that is easy to remember and explains what you are about.

☐ At your first meeting it will be important to set out how often you wish to host meetings and discuss everyone's desired level of involvement and their skills.

☐ Set up a way of staying in touch with members in between meetings. This could be as simple as an email form, Facebook group or online workspace.

☐ Look to festivals or other events where you can officially 'launch' your group. For example a local sustainability festival might offer a free tent for a community group. This way, more people will learn about you and you could possibly recruit more members.

☐ Let local radio, TV and newspapers know who you are with a media release detailing what you hope to achieve and invite them to your launch. The media is always looking for stories – yours could be the one they tell next.

☐ Never lose sight of your original goal but don't overburden the group to the point of burnout. Check in regularly to see how everyone is going and if they need help. And don't forget to celebrate the small wins; they are just as important as the big ones!

BAN THE BAG

Three years ago, I received a message in my inbox from some very experienced environmental campaigners. They invited me to help start up a statewide campaign to ban plastic bags in Victoria. At first I was nervous, feeling very unsure I had any skills to bring to the table apart from my passion for the issue. But, by this stage of my journey into reducing my own plastic use and living zero waste, I knew legislation would be one of the ways to get swift action. So I said yes, and Plastic Bag Free Victoria was formed.

The campaign's aim was to highlight and support local community efforts to stop the free distribution of single-use plastic bags while at the same time lobby the state government for a ban on the free distribution of single-use plastic bags. We put together a petition to present to the government demanding a ban on plastic bags and spent just under a year collecting over 10,000 physical signatures.

A campaign of this size required many volunteers with a variety of talents and skills. We relied on people to help spread the message online via social media, to email their local MPs and to stand on street corners asking for signatures. If people donated an hour a week or even just an hour a month, it all added up. Every time we asked someone for a signature we were talking about the issue and giving it urgency. We emailed and had meetings with those at different levels of government along the way, starting important conversations. I quickly saw how much of an impact a small group of people can make.

Our petition went on to be one of the largest delivered to our state parliament in a decade. But when a bill was first tabled for a ban on plastic bags, it was knocked back. We were disappointed, of course, but we didn't give up hope. Our efforts had added to the conversation, and soon, awareness spread further. Retailers began declaring they would put an end to handing out plastic bags, and a year later the state government declared they would put a ban on plastic bags, to come into effect in 2018.

ENGAGE WITH GOVERNMENT

Fact

In Rwanda, plastic bags are illegal – smuggling plastic bags can even incur a jail sentence.

One of the fastest ways to curb our plastic consumption problems would be through changing laws. A great example of this is the growing number of towns, cities, states and countries around the world declaring bans on plastic bags. Many of these decisions have been a direct result of lobbying by citizens.

There are many ways to engage with different levels of government. Your local council might have an advisory group or board that invites members of the public to join and help find solutions to reducing rubbish within the local municipality. Political representatives declare themselves available to talk with their constituents on any issues they are concerned about, so take advantage and set up a meeting to ask what could be done in your area. Don't be put off just because a political party as a whole might not support a particular idea – you could still find a sympathetic party member. You could challenge them to partake in Plastic Free July or start a compost in their office, or invite them to any events you might be holding. If they do get on board, even on a personal level, it can make a big statement and perhaps become a stepping stone towards them helping to fight for legislative change.

KEEP IT UP

You might think writing a letter, hosting a movie night or asking people to sign a petition won't amount to anything, but I have seen what is possible. There is a groundswell of people looking for a new way, where kindness, intention and responsibility reign, and treading lightly on this earth is normal. Just as I am writing this a friend has emailed me from Scotland to let me know they are set to ban plastic straws by the end of 2019. I truly believe that from knowing comes caring and from caring comes change. We can all be part of the story of change in our own way. I am aware I might not see a completely circular economy during my lifetime, but I'm not without hope that it will get there. And, when it happens, I know it will be because of people like you and me. Our actions, no matter their size, are always powerful. Never forget that.

DIRECTORY

Here are some suggestions for my favourite products and services, as well as some of the resources that inspired my *Waste Not* journey. The lists are by no means exhaustive, and my recommendations have a distinctly Australian flavour. I encourage you to do your own research and discover what is available in your area. There is a growing list of resources on my website too: therogueginger.com.

WHERE TO START

If you don't have easy access to a bulk, organic or health food store, there is a growing number of online businesses to help you stock up on necessities like scrubbing brushes or deodorant.

And Keep (UK)

Biome (AU)

Boobalou (UK)

Ecolosophy (AU)

Flora and Fauna (AU)

Going Green Solutions (AU)

Green Tulip (UK)

Less Plastic (UK)

Life Without Plastic (US)

Package Free Shop (US)

Shop Naturally (AU)

Tiny Yellow Bungalow (US)

Wild Minimalist (US)

Where to borrow or source second-hand online.

Craigslist
This American classifieds site is starting to expand around the world.

Ebay
The classic buy-and-sell site.

Facebook
Use the marketplace function and buy/swap/sell groups.

Gumtree
The Australian and UK websites are both great for buying, selling or renting items, as well as finding useful services such as repairs.

Open Shed (AU)
Hire tools, camping gear, sporting equipment – and put your own things up for hire!

The Freecycle Network
Join a group in your area to find or offer things for free!

Recycling can be confusing, but these websites will help you get it right.

Earth911 (US)

Electronics Take Back Coalition (US)

Recycling Near You (AU)

Recycle Now (UK)

Recycle.co.nz

TechCollect (AU)

Textile Recyclers Australia

KITCHEN + FOOD

These apps and websites can help you to find places that accept reusable containers for shopping or eating out.

Fair Food Forager

Responsible Cafes (AU)

Trashless Takeaway (AU)

Zero-Waste Home Bulk Finder

These websites have great tutorials to make food from scratch. YouTube is also good for cooking DIYs; look up Shakirah Simley's video on 'How to Make Homemade Pectin for Jam'. (While you're there, search 'Sewing Basics: How to make fabric napkins' and 'Fabric Scrap Dog Bed' to find a couple of my other favourite non-food-related tutorials.)

Food52
There are a couple of cooking basics tutorials I love on this website, including 'A Complete Guide to Nut, Seed & Grain Milks' and 'How to Make Alcoholic Ginger Beer from Scratch'.

Love Food Hate Waste
This website, run by the UK Waste and Resources Action Programme, has simple-to-follow low-waste recipes.

Further reading on kichen and food issues.

The Art of Fermentation by Sandor Ellix Katz

Ball Complete Book of Home Preserving by Judi Kingry and Lauren Devine

The Clever Cook by Sustainable Table (ebook)

Compost by Ben Raskin

One Magic Square by Lolo Houbein

Simplicious by Sarah Wilson, who also has great tips for cooking with scraps on her website: sarahwilson.com.

CLEANING + CARE

Fabric, Needlecraft and More (AU)
This not-for-profit sells fabric offcuts that would have ordinarily gone to landfill.

Ifixit
An online resource for repair manuals.

Repair Café
Find repair cafes all over the world.

Uplift Project (AU/NZ)
This organisation takes second-hand bras to distribute where they are needed.

These laundry powder brands come in cardboard boxes without plastic scoops.

Aware Environmental (AU)

EcoOver (UK)

Green Potions (AU)
I use Green Potions No. 5 as my stain remover

Meliora (US)

Tangie (US)

The Simply Co. (US)

Try your hand at up-cycling with these books to spark ideas.

Upcycling Crafts by Kitty Moore

ReMake It! by Tiffany Threadgould

The Art of Cardboard by Lori Zimmer

The Upcycled Toys Club by Matt Duncan

These Facebook groups are great places to connect with others and find ideas.

A Make Do and Mend Life (UK)

Up-Cycled Cloth Collective (UK)

Upcycle and DIY Australia

These websites and blogs help to discover brands that care about their creations as much as the earth.

Eco Warrior Princess (AU)

Ethical Clothing Australia (AU)

Ethically Kate (NZ)

EcoCult (US)

Fashion Revolution (AU)

Good On You

Saiint Sisters (UK)

Sustainability in Style (AU)

And these brands are saving fabric from landfill through their creations.

Good Day Girl (AU)

Reformation (US)

Study NY (US)

Tonlé (US)

The Very Good Bra (AU)

Zero Waste Daniel (US)

Or, instead of buying new, try hiring clothing for a big event.

Girl Meets Dress (UK)

Glam Corner (AU)

Rent the Runway (US)

Something Borrowed (AU)

The Runway Collection (US)

'Doing Laundry More Sustainably' by Dr Holly Kaye-Smith (who provided simple ways to reduce our need to wash our clothes so often in this book) – this report is available to read online.

BEAUTY + BODY

A lot of these makers sell through Etsy, which is a great place to search for zero-waste beauty and body products (as well as other zero-waste items such as beeswax wraps).

Beauty and the Bees (AU) Known for their great shampoo bars.

Black Chicken Remedies (AU) I recommend the Axilla Deodorant.

Clean-Faced Cosmetics (US)

Credo (US)

Dirty Hippie Cosmetics (AU) I'm currently using their concealer and lip/cheek stain.

Ethique (NZ) Ethique's waste-free beauty products have prevented more than 150,000 bottles from going into landfill. I am a big fan of their solid moisturising bars.

JuniperseedMerc (US)

Keeping it Natural (US) This store is where I buy my cake mascara. They will allow users to return packaging for refills.

Love Lula (UK)

Luna Zero Waste (UK)

Nourished Life (AU)

Wanderlightly (AU)

Zero Waste Beauty Australia (AU)

Period underwear is great for light flows or in conjunction with a mooncup or reusable pads.

Lunapads (US) As the name suggests, they also sell modern reusable pads, as well as mooncups and a range of leakproof underwear.

ModiBodi (AU)

Thinx (US)

These brands offer more sustainable floss options.

Dental Lace (US)

Eco-Dent (US)

The Aromatherapy Companion by Victoria H Edwards is a great book if you are interested in the art of aromatherapy and essential oils.

LITTLE PEOPLE + FURRY FRIENDS

BecoPets (UK)
Pet accessories made from recycled plastic.

BeeKeeper Backpacks (AU)
These school-friendly backpacks are made of up-cycled material, and each purchase helps provide education for children living in rural Cambodia.

Healthy Zero Waste Lunch Toolkit (AU)
The Government of Western Australia has provided this downloadable resource for schools.

Mason Bottle
We use the Mason Bottle nipple to convert our mason jars into baby bottles.

My Best Gift (AU)
Gift experience ideas for babies to teenagers.

Product Safety Australia
Check the model of second-hand baby items – or any second-hand items you're looking to purchase.

Pura Stainless (US)
The Kiki range is a stainless-steel bottle option with a changeable lid so that bottle can grow with baby.

Schools Recycle Right (AU)
Planet Ark has lesson plans for teachers on recycling.

Snappi (US)
These cloth nappy (diaper) fasteners are a great alternative to pins.

Tumbleweed Pet Poo Composter
A pet-poo-only compost bin if you'd rather not make your own.

Toy Libraries Australia
Look up a toy library or start your own.

These Facebook groups about cloth nappies (diapers), are endless resources.

MCN Reviews Uncensored (AU)

Clean Cloth Nappies Down Under (AU)

Buy and Sell your Modern Cloth Nappies (AU)

These websites have info pages on cloth nappies.

Waste Free With Kate (NZ)

Kelly's Closet (US)

Some useful further reading for parents.

Baby-Led Weaning by Gill Rapley and Tracey Murkett

Spit that Out! by Paige Wolf

Help children understand and learn about the effects of single-use plastics and waste through books and movies.

Books
A Bag and a Bird by Pamela Allen

All the Way to the Ocean by Joel Harper

Compost Stew by Mary McKenna Siddals

Lelani and The Plastic Kingdom by Robb N. Johnston

Sullie Saves the Seas by Goffinet McLaren

Film and TV
Wall E

The Lorax

The Wombles

FernGully

ENTER-TAINING + EVENTS

Furoshiki.com
Step-by-step guides to wrapping items using the traditional Japanese furoshiki method.

Kuttlefish
This online marketplace is dedicated to up-cycled goods – a great place for gifts, or just for inspiration. Pinterest is always great for inspiration too!

Merry-Go-Round (AU)
These cards come with a removable message insert, allowing recipients to keep the message and insert their own message before reusing for another time.

These businesses provide wine and beer refills in Melbourne, where I live, but they are part of a growing global movement. The CraftyPint.com also has a great list of locations to buy beer refills in Australia.

ReWine (AU)

Kegs on Legs (AU)

ON THE ROAD

Buy Eco Green (AU)
Sells many low waste and eco stationery items.

Catalogue Central (AU)
Instead of receiving paper catalogues, have them sent to your email.

Directory Select (AU)
Cancel your Yellow Pages or White Pages directories.

Green Collect (AU)
Find the best environmental solutions for office items that are the hardest to recycle.

Impact Travel Alliance
A global community and not-for-profit aimed at propelling the travel industry towards a more impactful future.

These brands offer portable water purifiers.

Grayl (US)

SteriPen (US)

These companies offer refillable markers and whiteboard markers.

Auspen (AU)

CopicMarker

ACT YOUR VISION

There are many groups on Facebook to help you connect with like-minded individuals, to learn more about zero-waste living and to share your own tips. I have listed only a handful of the larger groups here. However, most of them have links to smaller geographically based groups through their channels. To find others, simply type into Facebook search 'Zero Waste', 'Low Waste', 'Minimal Waste' or 'Plastic-Free' followed by your country or city name.

#WarOnWasteAU

Journey to Zero-Waste

Zero Waste + Plastic Free Living Perth (AU)

Zero Waste Heroes! (UK)

Zero Waste Minimalist

Zero Waste Tasmania (AU)

Zero Waste Victoria (AU)

To find people with like-minded views away from the internet, I suggest joining a clean-up group. Contact your local council for other groups in your area, or search on Meetup.com. The Australian Environmental Grantmakers Network also has a list of Australian environmental organisations.

Landcare Australia

Beach Patrol (AU)

Keep America Beautiful

Keep Britain Tidy

Sea Shepherd (AU)

Sustainable Coastlines (NZ)

Responsible Runners (AU)

FURTHER RESOURCES

Books

Bottlemania by Elizabeth Royte

Cradle To Cradle by Michael Braungart and William McDonough

Garbology by Edward Humes

Plastic Free by Beth Terry

Slow Death by Rubber Duck by Rick Smith and Bruce Lourie

Zero Waste Home by Bea Johnson

Junkyard Planet by Adam Minter

Make Garbage Great by Tom Szaky and Albe Zakes

Plastic: A Toxic Love Story by Susan Freinkel

The Story of Stuff by Annie Leonard

Film and TV

A Blue Ocean

A Plastic Ocean

Addicted to Plastic

Bag It

Clean Bin Project

Divide In Concord

No Impact Man

Plastic Paradise

The Story of Stuff

War on Waste (both UK and AU versions)

Waste Deep

A NOTE ABOUT THIS BOOK

During a workshop I facilitated on zero-waste living, I was talking with the attendees about the resources they found most useful in reducing waste. The overwhelming answer was the humble book: something they could have in the home for reference, and which could be lent to a friend to spark conversation.

While I have always been passionate about sharing my zero-waste lifestyle, it wasn't until becoming a new mum that I wanted to sit down and write a book. The future I envision for my son is one full of kind people, willing to help one another and take responsibility to ensure the next generation gets to enjoy this beautiful planet. I wanted to gather together everything I'd learned on my zero-waste journey to help make that future a reality.

I understand that writing a book can be a wasteful endeavour, and I thought long and hard about whether to do this instead of keeping everything electronic. But electronic products have an impact too – you would need to read quite a number of books on an e-reader before it became more sustainable than a physical book. I didn't set out to create a wasteful product but rather to share examples of how I have to learned to live a low-waste life for those perhaps not so plugged in to the digital world, or those who do still value the tangible resource of a book.

All efforts were taken to make this book a low-waste project. The editorial and design process was done almost entirely onscreen, and advanced reading copies were offered only electronically. Props for the shoot were sourced as sustainably as possible; for example, all the ceramics were locally hand-made. The entire book is printed on Forest Stewardship Council (FSC) certified stock. FSC is the highest standard forest certification scheme and the only one to be a member of ISEAL Alliance, the global association for sustainability standards. The paper is cut to size prior to printing in order to reduce wastage. The printing itself is in soy-based inks, which are more sustainable and produce less volatile organic compounds (VOCs) than their petroleum-based alternatives and makes it easier for the paper to eventually be recycled. All excess paper, plastic, wood and metal (such as printing plates) produced during the printing process will be recycled, as will any extra inventory (hopefully there isn't any!).

ACKNOWLEDGEMENTS

I'd like to acknowledge the first Australians and pay my respects to their elders past, present and emerging. The hundreds of nations that are now collectively called Australia lived a zero-waste lifestyle for much longer than I ever have, including the Wurundjeri-willam People of the Kulin nation, who looked after the country where I now reside in urban Melbourne.

Thank you to Arwen, Emily, Susan, Grace, Gavin, Stephanie and all the in-between folk at Hardie Grant who helped bring this book together. I appreciate your talent, patience, kindness and you asking me to write this book.

To my contributors and all-round excellent humans for their expert tips: Sabrina, Kirsty, Erin, Holly, Laura, Siska, Anamarie, Kirsten, Amanda and Jonathan.

Thank you to Victoria and family for opening up your home for the photoshoot while ours was under renovation.

Mum, thank you for looking after the baby, cooking meals and helping with the washing while I wrote most of this book. I couldn't have done it without your help. Dad, your words of encouragement in the beginning kept me going. To Adrienne and Andrew, thanks for always being there and listening to me. Family and friends, near and far, thank you for your continual support. My husband, The Builder, who didn't mind the kitchen being turned into a testing ground while I remade all the recipes I've used for years. Lastly, to my son: thank you for being patient with Mama while she wrote. I love you very much.

And to the people throughout history, who have used their voices and bodies to nurture and protect this planet, I recognise you and thank you.

ABOUT THE AUTHOR

Erin Rhoads has been writing about her zero-waste journey since 2013. Her blog, The Rogue Ginger, quickly became one of Australia's most popular eco-lifestyle websites, and Erin is now a prominent commentator on zero-waste living. She divides her time consulting with businesses on waste reduction, sharing skills and ideas at workshops and talks for kids and adults around Australia, and participating in environmental action groups.

Erin was a consultant on Australia's *War on Waste* and is a regular contributor on ABC Radio. She has been featured on BBC World, *The Project, Sunrise, The Age, The Guardian, The Australian Women's Weekly, Marie Claire, Peppermint* magazine and many more.

Erin lives in Melbourne, Australia, with her husband and son.

INDEX

Illustrations indicated in **bold**
DIYs indicated in *italics*

'WITH KNOWING COMES CARING, WITH CARING COMES CHANGE.'

CRAIG LEESON

Published in 2018 by Hardie Grant Books,
an imprint of Hardie Grant Publishing

Hardie Grant Books (Melbourne)
Building 1, 658 Church Street
Richmond, Victoria 3121

Hardie Grant Books (London)
5th & 6th Floors
52–54 Southwark Street
London SE1 1UN

hardiegrantbooks.com

A catalogue record for this
book is available from the
National Library of Australia

Waste Not
ISBN 978 1 74379 462 3

10 9 8 7 6 5 4 3

Publisher: Arwen Summers
Project Editor: Emily Hart
Editor: Susan Keogh
Design Manager: Jessica Lowe
Design and illustrations: Grace West
Photographer: Gavin Green
Stylist: Stephanie Stamatis
Production Manager: Todd Rechner

Colour reproduction by Splitting Image
Colour Studio
Printed in China by Leo Paper Product. LTD

This book was printed on paper certified
by the FSC™ and other controlled material